$ 144.90

MEXICO

120th anniversary
Berlitz®

Berlitz Publishing Company, Inc.

Princeton   Mexico City   Dublin   Eschborn   Singapore

How to use our guide

These 256 pages cover the **highlights** of Mexico. Although not exhaustive, our selection of sights will enable you to make the best of your trip.

 The **sights** to see are described between pages 39 and 193. Those most highly recommended are pinpointed by the Berlitz symbol.

The **Where to Go** section on page 36 will help you plan your visit according to the time available.

For **general background** see the sections The Land and the People (p8) and History (p20).

Entertainment and **activities** (including wining and dining) are recounted between pages 194 and 215.

The **practical information**, hints and tips you will need before and during your trip begin on page 216. This section is arranged alphabetically with a list for easy reference.

The **map section** at the back of the book (pp245–253) will help you find your way around and locate the principal sights.

Finally, if there is anything you cannot find, look in the **index** (pp254–256).

Printed in Switzerland by Weber S.A., Bienne.

2nd edition
Reprinted May 1998

CONTENTS

CONTENTS

Text: Don Allan
Staff Editors: Eileen Harr-Kyburz and Delphine Verroest
Photography: Adriano Heitmann
Cartography: Hardlines

Acknowledgements
We would like to thank Pamela Collins, Patricia Castro and the Mexican
Tourist Board, London.

*Found an error or an omission in this Berlitz guide? Or a change or new
feature we should know about? Our editor would be happy to hear from you.
Write to: Berlitz Publishing Company Ltd., Peterley Road, Oxford OX4 2TX,
UK. Be sure to include your name and address, since in appreciation for
a useful suggestion, we'd like to send you a free travel guide.*

*Although we have made every effort to ensure the accuracy of all the in-
formation in this book, changes occur incessantly. We cannot therefore take
responsibility for facts, prices, addresses and circumstances in general that
are constantly subject to alteration.*

Cover: A sculpture of the Chac-Mool, in Chichén Itzá (Adriano Heitmann).

UNITED

BAJA
CALIFORNIA
NORTE

SONORA

CHIHUAHUA

COAHUILA

BAJA
CALIFORNIA
SUR

SINALOA

DURANGO

ZACATECAS

NAYARIT

AGUASCALIENTES

JALISCO

GUAN

COLIMA

MICHOACÁN

MÉXICO
STATE

DISTRITO
FEDERAL

P A C I F I C

O C E A N

N

0 — 400 km

0 — 240 miles

6

NUEVO
LEÓN

TAMAU-
LIPAS

AN
UIS
POTOSÍ

QUERÉTARO
HIDALGO

TLAXCALA

*GULF OF
MEXICO*

YUCATÁN

VERACRUZ

PUEBLA

CAMPECHE

QUINTANA
ROO

GUERRERO

OAXACA

TABASCO

CHIAPAS

BELIZE

MORELOS

GUATEMALA

HONDURAS

EL SALVADOR

THE LAND AND THE PEOPLE

Mexico is a big, spectacular country with a distinctive character that is far more than the sum of its proud Indian and Spanish parts. On a land of great beauty and astonishing variety, Mexicans have created from these two stubborn strains a unique *mestizo* nation of mixed ancestry and genuinely original culture. Anything Mexican, from food and music to costumes and design, is instantly recognizable as such. The genius of modern Mexican artists can amaze and delight the visitor as much as traditional crafts and ancient stones.

'Of all that extensive empire which once acknowledged the authority of Spain in the New World, no portion for interest or importance can be compared with Mexico; and this equally whether we consider the variety of its soil and climate, the inexhaustible stores of its mineral wealth; its scenery, grand and picturesque beyond example; the character of its ancient inhabitants ... or lastly, the peculiar circumstances of its Conquest, adventurous and

romantic as any legend ...' These opening lines of William Prescott's magisterial history, *The Conquest of Mexico*, well express the country's dramatic impact. And they were written in the 19th century when so much of Mexico's treasures were still inaccessible or undiscovered.

The land is huge, roughly as big as Western Europe. Mexico's 88 million make it the world's largest Spanish-speaking nation. Metropolitan Mexico City, 65km (40 miles) across and home for some 20 million, is the biggest city on earth, with all the fascination and problems that come with it. It is the Western Hemisphere's oldest capital, founded by the Aztecs in 1325.

The land curves like a tunnel and is creased by ridge upon ridge of mountains. When Emperor Charles V

Multi-faceted Mexico: the grandeur of Chichén Itzá and the warmth of the Mexican people.

asked Cortés what his new dominions were like, the conquistador is said to have crumpled a piece of paper, tossed it on the table, and replied 'Like that.' More than half of Mexican territory is above 1,000m (3,000ft). Between the lofty ranges of the Sierra Madre Occidental and Oriental, a plateau tilts upward, first in arid lands, then into the fertile Central Highlands, culminating in the Valley of Mexico, once the heart of the Aztec empire.

Mexico City, at 2,450m (7,350ft), is ringed by snowcapped extinct volcanoes including Popocatépetl ('Smoking Mountain' to the Aztecs) and Iztaccíhuatl ('Sleeping Lady'). This is part of a volcanic rift crossing the country where the funnel narrows and the two Sierras come together in a tangle of ridges and ravines. Here a clash of plates in the earth's crust from time to time makes the land shudder and volcanoes rumble. Beyond this rift, in the low-lying Isthmus of Tehuantepec, the Gulf of Mexico and the Pacific Ocean are so close – only 201km (126 miles) apart – that it has been considered for a canal a number of times. (A railway was built instead, but the Panama Canal took the business.) Beyond the isthmus the land rises again to the Guatemalan border in the rain-forested mountains of Chiapas, ancient Mayan territory.

Two major peninsulas and some islands complete Mexico's geography. Narrow and mountainous Baja California on the Pacific extends 1,230km (764 miles) below the US border and is separated from the mainland by the Sea of Cortés, also known as Gulf of California, one of the world's greatest game fishing grounds. The Yucatán Peninsula is a flat pan of dry jungle jutting between the Gulf of Mexico and the Caribbean, where the palm-fringed islands of Cancún, Cozumel and Isla Mujeres are sheltered by a great barrier reef. Inland Yucatán is the site of magnificent Mayan ruins, still evoking their unsolved mystery. Mexico is world famous for coastal resorts, such as Acapulco and Cancún, but along its 9,655km shoreline are countless superb beaches.

Within this geographical framework are many contrasting landscapes, far removed from the misleading stereotype of Mexico as an expanse of cactus and sand – perpetual snowfields, pine woods, rolling ranchland and rich farms growing winter fruit and vegetables for export to the north, groves of coconut and bananas, mile-deep canyons and dense rainforest jungles. Climate differs widely too, depending both on latitude and altitude. Rain, or rather the lack of it, has been a constant preoccupation from time immemorial. Great temples were raised to the rain god and

The extinct volcano of Iztaccíhuatl ('Sleeping Lady'), watches over Mexico City.

priestly 'weathermen', with the help of intricate calendars and astronomy, aimed to harmonize planting times with the rains. Broadly speaking, it rains between May and October and is fair the rest of the year. Along the Pacific, the showers fall in the afternoon or at night, leaving hours of sunshine. The Caribbean and Gulf get heavy autumn storms and the jungles of Chiapas receive up to 3m (10ft) of rainfall during the year, while Baja California remains bone dry. Temperatures are high on the coast but relieved by steady breezes; a year-round spring climate reigns in the flowery Central Highlands. Mexico City, despite its altitude, is generally mild, sunny and dry, with intermittent summer rains and some chilly, smoggy days in winter.

There are, in fact, many Mexicos – racially, regionally, economically and culturally different, yet wholly Mexican. The majority of the population are *mestizo*, with varying mixtures of Spanish and Indian ancestry. In no other country of Latin America, and perhaps the modern world, has the confrontation of two races produced so thorough a merging as it has in Mexico. (Actually, three races are represented: tens of thousands of African slaves were brought over and assimilated in the 16th and 17th centuries.) This mix means that the average Mexican is descended both from the conquerors and from the conquered, a split that results in some ambivalent attitudes.

Cancún, in Quintana Roo, is the perfect holiday spot in Mexico.

There are no statues to Cortés, the victor of the Conquest, but plenty to Cuauhtémoc and other Indian leaders. The cultures of antiquity are venerated, but today the majority of pure Indians are at the bottom of the economic and social scale.

Machismo, the swaggering emphasis on masculinity, and the strict rules of chaste conduct for women are analysed by some psychologists as a reaction of the Mexican's collective memory of the rape of his female Indian ancestors by his male Spanish forebears. The *mañana* syndrome resists planning ahead and is linked to the fatalistic ancient belief that if the gods decide everything, planning is useless. Acceptance of strong leaders and a hierarchical structure of society and government has roots in pre-Conquest customs. The past is very much alive in the outlook of Mexicans and is the cement that binds diverse people together as a nation.

To say that some 20 per cent of the population are Indians gives no idea of the physical and cultural differences between, say, the short, stolid Maya with their oriental eyes

Reading Mexico
The adventure of discovering Mexico has inspired writers from Cortés him-
self up to the modern novelists and historians. Mexican literature adds
another dimension to understanding the country and its people. A short read-
ing list would include:

Historia Verdadera de la Conquista de la Nueva España *by Bernal Díaz*
del Castillo, who accompanied Cortés and an earlier expedition as well.
Vivid eye-witness account of the Conquest.

The Conquest of Mexico *by William Prescott. The classic history.*

2 Rabbit, 7 Wind: Náhuatl Poems *by Toni de Gerez. Moving ancient texts*
in translation.

Many Mexicos *by Lesley Bird Simpson, covering the history up to mod-*
ern times in a lively style.

Incidents of Travel in Yucatán and Chiapas *by John Lloyd Stephens. The*
19th-century adventures of the American who discovered many ruins, with
drawings of how they looked at the time.

Novels by 'B. Traven', the nom de plume of a mysterious German whose
adventure stories in authentic Mexican rural settings have been made into
many movies, including The Treasure of the Sierra Madre *and* The Wages
of Fear.

The Feathered Serpent *by D.H. Lawrence. An idiosyncratic but poetic*
evocation of the impression that Mexico made on Lawrence during his stay
in the 1920s.

The Children of Sanchez *by Oscar Lewis. An anthropologist's readable*
dissection of the lives of the poor in Mexico City.

The Labyrinth of Solitude, *the best known work of the poet-essayist-jour-*
nalist-diplomat Octavio Paz, who won the 1990 Nobel Prize for Literature;
it deals with the Mexican soul and its contradictions.

Where the Air is Clear *by Carlos Fuentes. Any title by Fuentes, Mexico's*
foremost novelist, will be rewarding both as an entertaining read and as
an introduction to Mexican attitudes.

Distant Neighbors *by Alan Riding, explains modern Mexico as seen by*
a journalist who covered the country for many years.

Under the Volcano *by Malcolm Lowry. Cuernavaca is the setting for this*
classic novel of a man's disintegration.

There is no shortage of specialized books on Mexican art, culture, ar-
chaeology, mythology, politics and history. Mexican literature in the
classic works of such writers as Sor Juana Inés de la Cruz, José
Vasconcelos, Emilio Rabasa, Juan Rulfo and Agustín Yáñez has achieved
international recognition. Contemporary Mexican novelists Gustavo Sainz
and Arturo Azuela reveal the stresses in the lives of the present generation
in the world's biggest city.

and curved noses, and the lean, leathery Tarahumaras of the Copper Canyon, who run for days at a time for sport. In the 16th century, over 200 Indian languages and dialects were identified; 58 are still spoken today. Even the Tzotzil Indians at San Cristóbal de las Casas turn to stare when the forest-dwelling Lacandón, with their shaggy hair and homespun white costume, come loping into town to sell monkey skins, birds and arrows. Each Indian group has its handicraft specialty in weaving, embroidery, copperware, pottery, basketry, carved wood, papier-mâché and lacquer, painting on bark paper, and much else that makes each village market a discovery and Mexico a paradise for shopping.

The monuments of antiquity in this country are wonders of the world. Awe-inspiring pyramids, beautiful sculpture, brilliant frescoes, exquisite jewellery and ceramics, as well as complex systems of measuring time and astral movements, testify to the skills of civilizations that flowered and then, for reasons still unfathomed, disappeared. Archaeologists continually revise their theories as more temples and entire cities are unearthed all over the country. For the tourist, discovering the treasures of pre-Colombian art in Mexican museums can be equally thrilling.

Colonial cities have a completely different appeal. Indian artisans added their own flourishes to Spanish baroque, producing a uniquely Mexican style for lavish churches and mansions built with Indian labour and the wealth of Mexico's mines and plantations. Cobblestone streets and the flower-filled balconies of houses with red-tiled roofs, wrought iron grilles and pastel walls preserve a 17th- and 18th-century atmosphere. Colonial Spain's influence pervaded Mexican life, but never overwhelmed it: the end result is still Mexican.

The same can't be said for the ultra-modern seaside playgrounds that pull in a big share of the 6 million visitors to Mexico each year. They are international and a huge success.

Every city and town, including the resorts, has a *zócalo*, or central plaza, and each is a stage where regional music is played in the evenings, families parade and the special character of the community is revealed. Mexico City's is a vast vacuum, a monument to all that is missing where Moctezuma's city stood. Acapulco's is a pocket of green shade, a refuge from the sun. In Veracruz an atmosphere of constant carnival throbs under its white arcades, while in Morelia the zócalo is patrician, somewhat austere, walled by colonial palaces.

Regional cooking can be a revelation, too, using fruits, vegetables

Overleaf: Mexico City's Zócalo, with the cathedral in the foreground.

and sauces rarely seen outside Mexico. Based on ancient recipes, it is full of surprises, such as the green pumpkinseed *pipián verde* sauce of Mérida, or Puebla's turkey with *mole poblano*, a sauce of bitter chocolate and 24 spices – a far cry from the hackneyed 'chile' served north of the Río Grande.

These aspects of Mexico seem unchanging, but the country is far from a quaint backwater. The economy is now driven by industry – automobiles, steel, glass and chemicals are manufactured and Mexico has the world's fourth largest reserves of petroleum. It continues to be first in silver mining and a leader in production of other minerals. Exports of seafood, fruits and vegetables are big business. Tourism earns 3 billion US$ a year. Political leaders these days are university-trained managers, not generals.

Villas behind high walls in city suburbs and yachts anchored off coastal resorts are evidence that the rich in Mexico are very rich indeed (the hallowed 1910 Revolution and a nominally socialist government notwithstanding). Considerably more evidence abounds that the poor are very poor – half of the country is unemployed or under-employed and the minimum wage is less than the equivalent of 4 US$ per day. One obvious problem is an exploding population: 51 million in 1970, 88 million in 1992. Another problem is the shortage of arable land. Farming still occupies over 30 per cent of the population, often following the primitive slash-and-burn techniques of their ancestors. Cutting the trees to clear marginal land for planting has caused disastrous erosion. Unfortunately, 80 per cent of the land is too steep or dry for agriculture – there just isn't enough good land to meet the needs of such a rapidly growing population. Land reform has tended to break up large estates into *ejidos*, small communal holdings inefficiently equipped, financed and worked. Mexico, where maize was first domesticated, now has to import this staple food.

Rural problems feed a migration to the cities that has swollen the capital into a mega-metropolis more than 65km (40 miles) across. Every day a thousand people at least leave the countryside and arrive in Mexico City in search of work, and another thousand are born there. Discouraging population growth and migration to the capital, modernizing agriculture, curbing inflation, providing housing, water and social services, and fighting pollution are the government's major priorities.

The government looks increasingly to tourism for revenue. Mexico's archaeological wonders and luxurious beach resorts are world renowned, but it's a big country and its natural and cultural attractions are far from over-exploited. There is much more *off* the beaten track than on it – in Mexico, discovery is still possible.

FACTS AND FIGURES

Geography: With an area of 1,987,183sq km (761,530sq miles) Mexico is about the size of Western Europe, or a quarter of the USA. The border with its northern neighbour is 3,326km (2,065 miles) long and it has a coastline of almost 9,500km (6,000 miles) along the Pacific Ocean and the Gulf of Mexico. On the south, it borders on Belize and Guatemala. The country extends from 32° in the north to 14° in the south, passing from the temperate to the tropical zone *en route*. The heartland is a high central plateau. It's a mountainous country, with half the territory over 900m (3,000ft) and volcanic peaks rising well above 5,000m (16,350ft) – the highest, Orizaba, reaches to 5,700m (18,640ft).

Population: 88 million in 1992, of whom about 70 per cent are *mestizo* (mixed European and Indian blood), 20 per cent Indian and 10 per cent Caucasian. 97 per cent are Roman Catholic.

Capital: Mexico City, with a population of 20 million for the metropolitan area.

Major cities: Guadalajara (3.5 million), Monterrey (3 million), Acapulco (2 million), Puebla (1.5 million), Tijuana (1.5 million).

Government: A Federal Republic, Estados Unidos Mexicanos, created under the Constitution of 1917 and composed of 31 states and the Distrito Federal, which includes the capital. The President is elected for six years, one term only. A Chamber of Deputies is elected for three years and a Senate for six years. The Partido Revolucionario Institucional has dominated politics since the 1930s.

Economy: 30 per cent of the population is engaged in agriculture, producing exports of coffee, cotton, fruit and vegetables, but the country has to import the staple food, maize, to meet its needs. Industry, such as manufacturing steel, automobiles, chemicals, textiles, clothing and assembling electronic parts for US manufacturers, occupies more than half the workforce. Per capita income is about $2,100 per year. Mexico is the world's fourth largest oil producer, with reserves of some 67 billion barrels. It leads the world in silver mining and is a leader in other minerals. Tourism attracts over 6.3 million visitors a year and earned $3 billion in 1989.

HISTORY

The history of Mexico embraces three themes – the rise and fall of Indian civilizations, the Conquest and 300-year colonial rule by Spain, and the tumultuous revolutions leading to independence with the evolution of a modern democracy.

This dramatic story begins some 50,000 years ago when a thick ice cap covering the northern top of the planet dried up the atmosphere and trapped rainfall, which lowered the level of the Bering Sea to expose a land bridge joining Asia and Alaska. Bands of primitive hunters from Siberia followed hairy mammoth and other big game across this strip; over thousands of years they worked their way southward. Campfire sites carbon-dated at 37500 BC. have been discovered along the way, and mammoth bones, together with stone-clad spear heads, have been unearthed not far from Mexico City. By 9000 BC the wanderers reached the farthest tip of South America. In this way, the Americas were populated by an Asiatic race that European explorers seeking a route to the East Indies later misnamed 'Indians'.

At the close of the Ice Age some 10,000 years ago, global warming melted the ice cap, the land bridge was submerged, migration ceased and the Americas were isolated to develop on their own. The big game gradually became extinct, but around 3500 BC the hunters in Mexico adapted by making a momentous discovery: an avocado pit or pumpkin seed stuck in the ground would grow and provide food. Next came the domestication of beans and a wild grass (maize), the staple foods of the region ever since. Agriculture meant settling down, and later on, the production of surpluses allowed tribes to support artisans and priests. By around 1200 BC a remarkable civilization began to emerge in the fertile lowlands beyond the Gulf Coast in what are now the Mexican states of Veracruz and Tabasco. Its founders were the **Olmecs**.

The Golden Age

Mystery shrouds the ancient history of Mexico. More than once, important centres were abandoned for reasons that remain obscure and entire peoples dispersed. The Olmec culture endured for more than a thousand years, then disappeared. In their prime, concurrent with the rise of classic Greece, the Olmecs developed the first writing in the Western Hemisphere (hieroglyphics that are still undeciphered), the first calendar and the first of the pyramidal structures so characteristic of Mexican antiquity. Without metal tools, the wheel or draught animals (unknown before the Conquest) the Olmecs carved portrait heads of their

A relic from the Golden Age of Mexican culture: a carved portrait head of an Olmec leader.

leaders from 40-tonne blocks of basalt transported long distances to their cities. Theirs was the 'mother culture' for all those that followed.

The Olmecs receded into the mists of history around 300 BC. The brilliant Maya had made their appearance in Guatemala and southern Mexico well before then, while in Oaxaca the Zapotecs had levelled a mountaintop to begin the series of constructions at Monte Albán later extended by the Mixtecs.

Dominating the central highlands, the Teotihuacanos, whose tribal identity is unknown, built the great

> ### The Ball Game
> *In the ball game, played in the ball court, players scored by batting or kicking a ball through rings high on the court walls. Hands couldn't be used. They must have tried desperately hard, for the price of defeat meant decapitation.*
> *But is that the right theory? Another school of thought argues that it was an honour and a privilege for the captain of the winning team to be beheaded – as a sacrifice to his God.*

pyramids and city of Teotihuacán, 'the place where gods become men'. It had an area of 11sq km, laid out in a grid with broad avenues, workshops and even hotels for visiting traders. By AD 550 its population of more than 100,000 made it one of the biggest cities on earth. Then it, too, fell – probably burned and pillaged by barbarian invaders – and it never recovered. It had been in ruins for more than 600 years by the time the Aztecs arrived in the 14th century.

The Golden Age of all these early Indian cultures was roughly between AD 300–900. Although of Asian stock, the tribes spoke unrelated languages and differed in appearance and temperament. They traded with each other and shared traditions, such as pyramid temples and the ritual 'ball game' played on courts in temple compounds. They used a bar-and-dot system of numbers, a 365-day calendar more exact than the one employed in Europe at the time, and created magnificent artworks in fresco painting, ceramics and sculptured clay and stone. Books were written in hieroglyphic characters on pounded bark paper. An elite class of priests and warrior nobles ruled a peasantry that provided labour for building the temples and growing food. Then, between AD 600–900, a series of calamities, perhaps prolonged droughts coupled with invasions of agressive tribes, caused many great centres to be abandoned.

The old civilizations were soon hard pressed by these more warlike peoples. First came the Toltecs of Tula and Cholula, who seem to have extended their influence into the Yucatán Mayaland, and then the Aztecs, who called themselves the Mexica. According to their legend, these nomads from the north had been told by the gods to make their home where they would see an eagle holding a serpent. The prophecy was fulfilled in 1325 in the Valley of Mexico by the shores of Lake Texcoco and a settlement was established on low islands. The eagle and serpent is now the emblem of the Mexican flag.

In less than a century the Aztecs made themselves masters of the valley. Their island capital became

An Aztec stone carving on display at the Museo de Antropología, in Mexico City.

Tenochtitlán, a monumental city criss-crossed by canals and linked to the mainland by causeways. They were not so much originators as developers of advanced civilization, taking on many of the customs of their more cultured predecessors. One of their own contributions was mastery of war.

By the start of the 16th century, the Aztecs controlled tribes from the Gulf of Mexico to the Pacific and as far south as present-day Guatemala, who were obliged to pay tribute to Tenochtitlán. Moreover, a principal object of Aztec raiding was to take prisoners. They believed that human sacrifices were required to bring the sun back each day from the underworld of darkness. A steady supply of captives was needed for this purpose.

In the end, these demands were the undoing of the Aztecs, for when the Spanish conquistadors arrived in 1519, vassal tribes welcomed them as deliverers from the hated overlords. But these Indians only exchanged one set of masters for a harsher one. Within a century, an estimated 75 per cent of the indigenous population of Central Mexico had been killed in battle, succumbed to imported diseases such as smallpox and measles, or died from slave-labour working conditions. Their temples were torn down and the stone used to build churches and Spanish palaces. Their books were burned and golden ornaments melted into ingots sent to Madrid. Their

leaders were killed and their women were mated to the invaders. The Conquest was not merely a seizure of territory, it was the eradication of a 3,000-year-old civilization, dating back to the Olmecs.

The Conquest
Within a decade of Columbus's last voyage in 1504, Balboa had reached the Pacific in Panama, but the very existence of a flourishing civilization in Mexico was still unsuspected. The first clue was brought back to Cuba in 1517 and 1518 by the expeditions of Francisco Hernández de Córdoba and Juan de Grijalva. They had skirmished with Maya in Yucatán and returned with some golden trinkets, two prisoners who served later as interpreters, and reports of a towered city (Tulum) they compared to Seville.

In 1519, Diego Velázquez, the Spanish Governor of Cuba, chose **Hernán Cortés** to organize an expedition to follow up these probes. Cortés had come to Cuba in 1504 at the age of 19 and had become a prosperous settler. He outfitted 11 ships and recruited more than 600 men with 16 horses and 14 small cannons. Thirty-two of the soldiers were equipped with crossbows and 13 with muskets. Such was the little band of adventurers who were to confront and conquer an empire of an estimated 5 to 6 million. Their first landfall was the island of Cozumel, where they acquired another interpreter – a Spanish priest who had survived a shipwreck years before and had been enslaved.

As the Spaniards sailed up the coast, they encountered hostile communities and fought skirmishes whenever they went ashore. They finally came to a harbour at the spot where Veracruz now stands. The day was Good Friday and the name of the city they later founded, 'the True Cross', commemorates the event. The harbour hinterland was controlled by the Aztec ruler, **Moctezuma**, but Cortés claimed the territory for Spain and called it Nueva España. He decided to strike inland, and to forestall any reluctance on the part of his men, he burned all of his ships on the beach except one

sent back to Cuba. With the help of **Malinche**, a captive princess presented to him as a gift by a defeated town, he avoided traps along the way.

On 8 November 1519, the little band of Spaniards beheld Tenochtitlán, the great city with a population estimated at over 300,000 set in its emerald lake. Moctezuma, carried royally in a litter and bearing gifts, came to meet Cortés. The Aztecs did not fight initially because the arrival of the fair and bearded

The port of Veracruz saw Cortés depart on his expedition against the Aztecs

Cortés fulfilled a prophecy – the long-awaited return of the god Quetzalcóatl who had sailed away in the dim past, promising to return one day from the East.

The king housed Cortés and his men in a mansion beside the great temple and near his own palace. In short order, Cortés took Moctezuma hostage and in subsequent riots, the king was killed by a stone flung by his own people – according to the Spanish version of the story. Meanwhile, Governor Velázquez had sent troops from Cuba to arrest Cortés, whose loyalty he mistrusted. Cortés returned to Veracruz and won over the expedition as reinforcements for his cause. But when they marched back to Tenochtitlán, they found their comrades besieged. Pedro de Alvarado, whom Cortés had left in charge, had massacred Aztec devotees during a religious festival in the great temple square, mistaking their inspired frenzy for a revolutionary uprising. The Spaniards were forced to flee the city, losing more than half their men and weapons as they fought their way out by night across a causeway to the mainland. Some, overloaded trying to carry out gold, drowned in the lake. This has been known ever since as the *Noche Triste*, or 'Night of Sorrow'.

The routed Spaniards ate their horses and lived on grass as they fought their way back to Veracruz. A year later, after building a flotilla of war canoes and with reinforcements

The architecture of this building in San Miguel de Allende bears all the marks of colonial influence.

from Cuba and 50,000 Indian allies, they returned to lay siege to the city, defended by Moctezuma's successor, Cuauhtémoc. Tenochtitlán fell on 13 August 1521, after a 90-day siege and the final battle in the suburb of Tlatelolco. With its head severed, the Aztec empire collapsed and the Conquest of Mexico was achieved.

King Charles I (Holy Roman Emperor Charles V) enobled Cortés as Marquis del Valle de Oaxaca, with a vast domain. According to custom, Cortés rewarded his followers with lands, '*en encomienda*', which included the native inhabitants as their property. But the king also removed Nueva España from control of the soldiers of fortune by sending a viceroy and bureaucrats to administer the new colony. One fifth of the wealth sent back to Spain was the royal share.

The church, too, sent missionaries to convert the Indians. Churches and convents were built where temples had stood. Zealous monks covered great distances on foot, and their accounts of Indian practices are some of the best records remaining, for Indian writing was destroyed as heathen. Only three books, called *codices*, survive today in European museums. A few priests, such as Bishop Bartolomé de

las Casas, protected Indians in their care from the worst savagery of the colonizers. (In fact, Indians accepted the powerful replacement of their vanquished gods and have become devout worshippers in a country that is now 97 per cent Roman Catholic.)

In the late 16th and 17th centuries, settlement of Nueva España proceeded rapidly. Mexico City, erected on the ruins of Tenochtitlán and enriched by huge silver deposits and plantations exploited with Indian labour, became a grand capital – proud, though still smaller and less brilliant than Moctezuma's. Other handsome cities grew near the mines, plantations and provincial centres where monastic orders acquired large properties. Indians did the work, adding flourishes to

Spanish baroque that makes Mexican church architecture wildly ornate.

The Spaniards brought in cattle, sheep and horses (only the turkey and dog were native to Mexico – even mice came from Europe), imported sugar cane, bananas and oranges. Mexico in return gave Europe tomatoes, maize, vanilla, avocados and chocolate. Acapulco became the trading port where galleons unloaded silks, ivory and porcelain from Asia, while from Veracruz other galleons carried gold and silver, semi-precious stones, sugar and tobacco to Spain. (English, Dutch and French pirates preyed on these treasure ships.)

By the early 1700s, out of a population of 6 million, there were only a few million pure Indians left and almost as many *mestizos* of mixed blood, dominated by a smaller class of well-to-do Spaniards born in Mexico called *criollos* and the *peninsulares*, or *gachupines*, administrators, churchmen and entrepreneurs born in Spain who alone were allowed to hold office, and so controlled all the positions of power. Friction grew between the privileged classes rooted in Mexico and those from Spain.

Meanwhile, back in Europe and North America the winds of change were shaking the old regimes. It wasn't long before agitation for independence began to spread throughout Mexico.

Independence and Revolution

The revolt started with *criollos* in the silver mining area who resented their exclusion from power and Spain's oppressive taxes. One of their leaders was a *criollo* village priest, **Father Hidalgo** of Dolores. When their plans were discovered, Hidalgo rang the church bell on 16 September 1810, defiantly proclaiming Mexico an independent republic. (The bell now hangs in the government palace in Mexico City.)

His Indian and *mestizo* flock grabbed pitchforks and machetes and went after the *gachupines*. The movement raced so quickly among the poorer classes, who burned and looted as they captured Guanajuato and other towns, that the *criollos* themselves felt threatened. Many abandoned this first revolt, which the Spanish authorities put down.

Hidalgo and the other plot leaders were executed.

But by this time the Indians and *mestizos* had seen what they could do. A *mestizo* priest, **José María Morelos**, rallied a peasant army of insurgents around causes that continued to ignite revolts into the 20th century: votes and equal rights for all, distribution of land to the landless, a republican government. Although Morelos was defeated and executed in 1815, back in Europe Spain had been liberalized and weakened under Napoleonic pressure and had neither the inclination nor the power to maintain the status quo in her colonies. Now even Mexican conservatives opted for an independence they felt they could control. The scattered insurgents united with the *criollos* to drive the Viceroy and Spanish troops from Mexico City on 27 September 1821.

Independence did not bring democracy or relief to the exploited classes. The military leader, General **Augustín de Iturbide**, declared himself Emperor Augustín I, setting a pattern of *coup d'état* and military dictatorship that persisted for years to come. Within a few months Iturbide was sent packing by another officer whose theatrical style characterized the chaotic decades

Maize, the staple food of Mexico, is inextricably linked with the history of the country.

following independence – **Antonio López de Santa Anna**. In the next 42 years Mexico had 58 presidents. Santa Anna had the job 11 times. When he lost his leg in a battle, he had it buried with full honours in an elaborate tomb.

In fact, Mexico was ill prepared for democracy and independence. For centuries Spain had bled the country of its wealth, investing next to nothing for its welfare. Society was split among grossly unequal classes with conflicting interests. The first Constitution established a federal republic with 18 sovereign states that became power bases for feudal warlords and landowners, including the biggest landowner of all, the church. And the reigning internal chaos made Mexico vulnerable to the dynamic westward expansion of the United States.

In 1836 Santa Anna marched north to confront Yankee settlers in Mexican Texas. He captured the fortified Alamo in San Antonio but soon afterward lost his army and was taken prisoner by Sam Houston at the Battle of San Jacinto. Mexico never recognized independent Texas when it became a US state in 1845, and broke off diplomatic relations with America then. Following skirmishes over disputed territory,

Detail from Diego Rivera's mural depicting everyday life of Mexicans in Tenochtitlán.

General Winfield Scott landed 10,000 men at Veracruz and took Mexico City. Cadets at the military academy in Chapultepec Castle fought the American troops to their death and are immortalized as the *niños héroes*, or 'boy heroes'.

Under the Treaty of Guadalupe Hidalgo, the US took most of Arizona, New Mexico, Colorado and California – half of Mexico's territory – paying $15 million blood money in return. A further strip of 103,600sq km (40,000sq miles) in Arizona and New Mexico was picked up for $10 million in 1853 (the 'Gadsden Purchase'), sold by Santa Anna to raise funds for an expanded army and stave off bankruptcy. Two years later a mob in the capital revolted against his profligate dictatorship and Santa Anna finally fled to exile for the last time.

At this low point in Mexico's history the Liberals, representing the dispossessed Indians and *mestizos*, drafted a new Constitution in 1857 which, among other things, prohibited slavery and removed the privileges of the Church. It separated state and church powers and established a civil registry for births, marriages and deaths, as well as secular schools. The Conservatives, made up of the *criollos*, landowners, and the military and religious establishment, resisted. And the Pope declared excommunication for any Catholic signing these reforms. Once again the countryside became a battlefield.

31

The Monumento a la Revolucíon – that of 1910 – looms over the Plaza de la República.

Out of the turmoil emerged one of Mexico's greatest figures, **Benito Juárez**. Juárez was a Zapotec Indian orphaned at three, who did not speak Spanish until the age of 12. Educated for the priesthood in Oaxaca, he turned to law and in time became governor of the state and drafter of the anticlerical provisions of the 1857 Constitution. When the Liberal fighters defeated the Conservative forces, Juárez was confirmed as President in 1861, ready to carry out La Reforma, the reforms embodied in the Constitution.

The drama unfolded. With the National Treasury empty, Juárez had suspended payment on all foreign debts. Spain, Britain and France had debt claims against Mexico (one was the bill of a French pastry chef) and proposed to seize Mexican ports until these were satisfied. Napoleon III, encouraged by Mexican Conservatives, wanted to go farther and to install a monarch to govern the unruly country. Spain and Britain balked at this, but France invaded anyway. The French were beaten at Puebla on 5 May 1862, but Napoleon III increased his invasion force and by 1864 held the capital and crowned an Austrian prince as Emperor Maximilian I. Juárez, moving from refuge to refuge in a simple black carriage that has

Murals are a popular means of expression in Mexico. Here, a fresco gives homage to the nation's heroes.

become his symbol, kept on fighting in the provinces.

Maximilian and Empress Carlotta moved into Chapultepec Castle, former residence of the viceroys, and set about recreating Europe in Mexico City. A broad tree-lined avenue modelled on the Champs-Elysées was laid out. Court entertainments distracted the puppet monarch, who never understood why he was not loved by 'his people'. But when the US Civil War ended, Washington was able to support Juárez. In 1867, Napoleon III withdrew French soldiers, more needed in Europe. Abandoned, Maximilian was soon captured and shot by a firing squad. Ten years after promulgating his reforms, Juárez was able to apply the laws sequestering the property and

sharply restricting the activities and revenues of the Church. Formal relations with the Vatican remained severed until 1990.

The Reforma was followed by the Porfiriato. **Porfirio Díaz**, a general who had helped rout the French at Puebla, seized power in 1876 and held it as dictator for 35 years. His famous remark, 'Poor Mexico, so far from God and so near to the United States,' was odd, coming from him – Díaz brought in North American investors who built railways, modernized mining, extended

---

United American Trade

The proposed free-trade zone, uniting 362 million people of Mexico, the US and Canada in a common market, may be the nucleus of what President Bush has called an economic bloc in the Americas 'from Point Barrow to Patagonia'. This is just what Mexico's President Salinas has been advocating since his election in 1990.

The Harvard-trained economist's aim is to attract industry to Mexico, where 87 per cent of the plentiful workforce is not only literate and capable but also ten times cheaper than north of the border.

Mexican labour is cheaper, too, than in the Pacific Rim countries which have prospered making clothing and assembling electronic products for the US. Why shouldn't Mexico, a good neighbour, get the business? asks President Salinas.

Already more than half a million Mexicans are employed in some 1,800 assembly plants, maquiladora, along the border that separates the 'First World' from the 'Third'. Workers come from all over the country in search of jobs; they live in shanty towns that have sprung up in the last 25 years from Tijuana to Matamoros; border towns like Nogales and Ciudad Juárez have become major centres.

Earning an average of $5 a day, these workers turn out auto components, TV sets, computers, clothing and countless other goods that are put together with US parts and shipped back for sale by major US corporations. Maquiladora operations are second only to oil as dollar-earners in Mexico's $52-billion trade with its big neighbour.

---

electricity, discovered oil and allowed the dictator to balance the budget. Don Porfirio loved ostentation and all things European. Ornate opera houses and public buildings proliferated in the cities. He was not a benevolent despot, however. As the rich got richer, the poor got poorer still, and when they became restive, they were shot down by a new federal police force, the *rurales*. Lands assigned to Indian communities in colonial times were seized. Peasants were forced to work seven days a week as virtual slaves because of debts owed to landowners. Two per cent of the population owned nearly 100 per cent of the land.

The country seethed with an undercurrent of rage that burst out in the **Revolution of 1910** with uprisings in the north led by the bandit **Pancho Villa**, and in the south by the Indian agrarian reformer **Emiliano Zapata**, with **Francisco I. Madero** as their political mentor. Díaz was persuaded to resign and retire to France. Madero was elected President, but fell victim to the old pattern of *coup d'état* and was shot. Villa and Zapata went on the rampage, while the heir to legitimacy, President **Venustiano Carranza**, played all sides. Local warlords fought battles of their own. Haciendas were burned, banks looted, trains blown up and the country split into fratricidal factions. In ten years, close to 2 million Mexicans died in the violence.

In 1916 the US sent a detachment under General John Pershing in a futile attempt to capture Villa after he had raided over the border. In a third invasion from the North, US marines again seized Veracruz in an overreaction to a trivial incident. Zapata was murdered in 1919, Carranza in 1920 and Villa in 1923. A true revolution had nevertheless been achieved. A new Constitution proclaimed that the land and everything underground belonged to the people. The President was barred from reelection after a six-year term. Labour unions were authorized. Priests were to be limited to one per 100,000 population and could not wear clerical habits outside the church. All public education was made secular. For several years thereafter priests refused to say mass as a protest and, in a final burst of violence, the **Cristero Rebellion** pitted religious militants against government troops in the central highlands and Yucatán.

The custodian of the revolution's goals was a movement founded in 1929 which has evolved into the present majority Partido Revolucionario Institucional (PRI). It has governed Mexico ever since. There have been very different regimes, all theoretically Socialist. In 1936, President **Lázaro Cárdenas** nationalized the railways, introduced land reform programmes, and expropriated the holdings of foreign oil companies – and the *peons* started to get land. Cárdenas was followed by leaders who developed Mexican industry during World War II and tourism in the post-war years. Demonstrations against conservative trends in government in 1968 ended with police shooting down protesters. The same year, Mexico City hosted the Olympic Games.

In the 1970s and 1980s, petroleum reserves discovered in the Gulf area were estimated at 67.6 billion barrels, making Mexico the world's fourth largest oil producer. The country borrowed heavily against these reserves for development but got caught short when oil prices fell. Instead of riches, Mexico was saddled with a debt of over $100 billion. After his election in 1988, President **Carlos Salinas de Gortari** carried out austerity measures that led world banks to renegotiate the debt. He contributed to the new 'clean' image of Mexico when he started getting rid of corrupt labour leaders and other profiteers, as other parties won state and local elections, and for the first time in more than 60 years seemed to present the ruling party with a challenge.

WHERE TO GO

Where to go in Mexico depends on your dreams. For sun-seekers there are 6,000 miles of coastline. Along these glorious beaches you can take your pick of sybaritic resort hotels serving steak, lobster and other refined fare by candlelight, or head for an offbeat hideaway where you can sleep in a hammock by the beach and catch your own lobster in water as clear as glass.

For art enthusiasts and cultural explorers there are the incomparable treasures of 'lost' civilizations in great museums and some 13,000 archeological sites, including the famous pyramids near Mexico City and the mysterious abandoned cities of the Maya. The heritage of 300 years of Spanish colonization, embellished with native Mexican exuberance, lives on in the cobblestone streets of picturesque cities and towns. In the countryside are Indian communities where traditional lifestyles have survived almost unchanged over the centuries.

The shopper and collector will find a bonanza of handcrafted silver, ceramics, textiles and leather goods in colourful village markets. For the sports mad there's diving off a barrier reef second only to Australia's, world-class fishing for marlin, sailfish and other big game trophies, and huge flocks of wintering geese and duck to hunt. Nature lovers can witness the migration of thousands of whales to their Baja California breeding grounds and marvel at millions of monarch butterflies clustered in a forest at the end of their flight from Canada.

In season, top matadors perform in the country's bullfight arenas, there's betting and thrills at racetracks and at *jai-alai* (the fast-moving Basque court game), and at all times plenty of golf, tennis and riding in reliable sunshine. The diversity of regional music and dancing will surprise those whose knowledge stops with *La Cucaracha*, just as the range and delicacy of Mexican cuisine will delight anyone dreading the ubiquitous *chile con carne*, a Texan invention, in fact.

Mexico City was already the brilliant centre of an Aztec empire much more populous than Spain when the dazzled Spanish conquistadors 'discovered' it in 1519. Today, it combines the allure of a sophisticated modern capital, with masterpieces of urban architecture, luxury hotels, fine restaurants and shops, and the fascination of a living theatre where all the episodes of a turbulent past are represented and history continues to be made.

So where to begin? The majority of foreign visitors to Mexico head for the beach resorts, such as Acapulco and Puerto Vallarta on the Pacific, or

When in Mexico, you are bound to come across a festival or fiesta, such as this one in Oaxaca.

Papier-mâché is a favourite art form in Mexico. This sculpture, overlooking the capital, is by Pedro Linares.

Cancún and Cozumel on the Caribbean. Since these are served by direct flights from abroad, many beach-bound tourists never see the rest of the country. This is a shame, for discovering the variety of Mexico is a rewarding experience quite easy to arrange.

All the main centres are linked by air, rail and first-class bus service. Car rental agencies abound. With a little planning you can cover the capital and the pyramids, and still get a nice tan at the beach in a fortnight. Or sample highlights of the whole enchilada in three weeks. A complete tour requires a lot of time: remember, this is one big country.

Starting for convenience with Mexico City and its nearby attractions, we have described side trips and regional itineraries: Cuernavaca–Taxco–Acapulco; Indian Oaxaca and its coast along with the state of Chiapas; Mayaland, which includes Yucatán, Cancún and Cozumel; the colonial Silver Cities; Guadalajara and its hinterland as well as the Pacific Coast resorts; Copper Canyon in the north and Baja California; and finally Veracruz and the Gulf of Mexico. Whether your first trip to Mexico is for two weeks or ten, there's so much to marvel at that you're likely to come back for more.

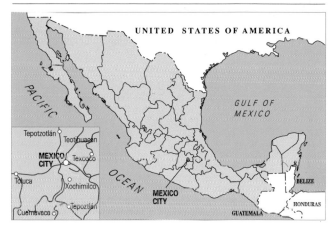

MEXICO CITY

South of the Río Grande, when people talk about 'Mexico', they mean Mexico City. The capital is centre stage for all aspects of national life – political, financial, intellectual and social. It is a magnet that has drawn nearly one out of five Mexicans to its 350 sprawling *colonias*, the elegant suburbs, crowded neighbourhoods and ramshackle squatter settlements that hold an estimated 20 million souls. Big as it is, Mexico City is not a metropolis that overpowers. Its inhabitants, nicknamed *Chilangos* by the rest of the country, put up with the frustrations of urban crowding with consistent courtesy and good humour. Most of its attractions for the tourist are easy to visit and spacious. They lie along the 3-mile axis between the **Bosque de Chapultepec** park and the **Zócalo**, two hubs joined by the splendid, tree lined Paseo de **la Reforma**. The many excellent hotels catering to visitors are found here or are within walking distance.

The size of the city is most impressive seen from the air. Approaching the airport, your plane crosses the high mountains that encircle the saucer-shaped Valley of Mexico, and then descends rather sharply to land. By day, you may feel as though you're plunging into a brown sea. That's the smog from factories and some 3 million vehicles. Take a good look at the volcanoes, **Popocatépetl** and **Iztaccíhuatl** –

39

from the ground you may never see them through the smog. As you circle the airport the city stretches out in all directions. You can spot small volcanic craters cradling farms in their fertile ash and the outline of the great lake, now mostly drained and built upon, that surrounded the Aztec city.

Unless you hit the rush hours, the ride in from Benito Juárez Airport takes no more than half an hour on the expressway. You'll spot the dark bronze Pemex Tower with its nailhead top, the 42-storey Torre Latinoamericana flashing the time and some other modest skyscrapers. The dome that looks like a giant tortoise is a sports arena. The expressway around the city is the **Periférico**. Main exits are to avenues marked as *ejes*, or axes, which run from the periphery to central zones. The city streets, as in most Mexican cities and towns, form a grid – a pattern introduced by Spain in colonial times. Mexicans thwart this orderly layout by changing some street names every few blocks to honour a long list of national heroes. Rare is the town that does not have streets named Juárez, Morelos, Hidalgo, and Insurgentes.

Mexico City's neighbourhoods have clusters of 'theme' street names. The **Zona Rosa**, the district of boutiques, hotels and restaurants midway up the Reforma, for example, has streets named after cities; on the other side of the avenue are river names. In

The Zócalo: face on, the Palacio Nacional and, on the left, the Catedral Metropolitana.

the old town, around the Zócalo, are the country names, while mountains are the feature of the Lomas de Chapultepec suburb. Other *colonias* commemorate poets, statesmen, scientists, and so on. Thus a street's name often will indicate its location.

Getting around is no problem. The metro covers the city with nine lines and 125 stations. Some attractive stations also function as centres for shopping and socializing. One, Pino Suárez, is built around part of an Aztec temple; another, Bellas Artes, posts art exhibitions; the sunken plaza of the Insurgentes station is a showcase. The French-built metro is clean, fast and almost soundless. Above ground, taxis are plentiful and inexpensive, while *colectivos* and *peseros* (privately operated minibuses and vans that cruise fixed routes and stop on demand), supplement a network of public yellow buses that offer one of the world's cheapest rides.

To get the feel of the place, however, you may want to sign up for one of the many city bus tours advertised in hotels and travel agencies. A good starting point is the Zócalo, the point from which all national highways measure their distance.

The Zócalo

The official name of this central square is the Plaza de la Constitución. An equestrian statue of Spain's King Carlos IV once stood here. It was removed after independence, but its pedestal, or *zócalo*, remained for some years and became a popular meeting place. Now central plazas all over Mexico are informally called 'the zócalo'.

The vast, unadorned square (240m or 792ft to a side) covers the very centre of what used to be Tenochtitlán, the city the Aztecs founded in 1325. With its solitary flagpole and the sombre shades of the surrounding buildings, it has a lingering air of melancholy. On holidays, decked out with coloured lights and stages for bands and dancers, it is filled with crowds – otherwise, the emptiness evokes everything that is missing from this space. If all the Aztec building blocks of *tezontle* (wine-coloured lava) were to be returned by magic to their original locations, the Zócalo would reappear as a teeming Indian market beneath brightly painted pyramids and palaces. Here is how Bernal Díaz del Castillo, one of Cortés's soldiers, described it:

'We were astounded at the great number of people and the quantities of merchandise ... dealers in gold, silver and precious stones, feathers, cloaks, and embroidered goods, and male and female slaves ... chocolate merchants ... those who sold sisal cloth and ropes and the sandals they wear on their feet ... Then there were the fruit sellers, and the women who sold cooked food, flour and honey cake and tripe ... pottery of all kinds ... timber, boards, cradles, beams, paper and some reeds that smell of liquidamber and are full of tobacco ... Some of our soldiers who had been in many parts of the world, in Constantinople, in Rome and all over Italy, said that they had never seen a market so well laid out, so large, so orderly and so full of people.'

Much as the *conquistadores* admired Tenochtitlán, they demolished it totally, filled in the canals to make streets and used the Aztec stone to build Mexico City. They called the open centre the Plaza de Armas, a military parade ground. The **Catedral Metropolitana** and **Sagrario** (sanctuary) close the north end of the square. The cathedral was begun in 1573, and by the time the towers were completed in 1813 it incorporated the styles of many ar-chitects and artists, inside and out. The north and west sides reflect the austerity of 16th-century Castille; baroque and neoclassical elements appear in the main, southern façade; rococo breaks loose in some of the interior chapels, notably the **Altar de los Reyes**. This 'Altar of the Kings' in the apse, is an intricate concoction of carved wood covered with gold leaf, harbouring many a hand-wringing saint with eyes cast heaven-ward, and paintings darkened by age and smoke.

The cathedral is big, as befits its site and role, and incorporates 51 domes, including the central cupola designed by **Manuel Tolsá**. Many of the 14 chapels were damaged in a 1967 fire and are still being restored. The second on the right holds the black **Cristo del Veneno** (Christ of the Poison). Details vary, but basic legend has it that a local bishop who had been poisoned was saved when he kissed the image, which drew out the venom, shrivelled up and turned black. The last chapel on the left is dedicated to San Felipe de Jesús, the first Mexican saint, who was mar-tyred in 1597 attempting to convert the Japanese. It also contains the ashes of Augustín de Iturbide and the throne on which he was crowned emperor.

Tilting away from the Cathedral on the right is **El Sagrario**, dedicated in 1768 to Santiago (St James), the patron saint of Mexico City. The two façades and finely carved doors of this smaller church are considered masterpieces of Churrigueresque, the extravagant baroque style of the Spanish architect **José Churriguera** adopted and adapted throughout 18th-century Mexico. It features Renaissance elements, such as inverted obelisks, Greek columns and pilasters, garlands and cornices, often tumultuously assembled and leaving no space empty.

The two churches, like a number of others in the central district, have been sinking and sagging for years. Draining the surrounding lake and pumping water have caused the slow collapse of the land on which they 'floated'. In fact, this flexibility has probably saved the buildings from damage during earthquakes. They are now supported by pilings. Beside the Sagrario, a model of Tenochtitlán sits in a basin of water that represents Lake Texcoco. Here the three causeways linking the island city with the land joined at the ceremonial centre of Moctezuma's empire. The sacred enclosure was 45m square (500ft square) and held 78 buildings, including the Royal Palace.

Just beyond the Sagrario a wall encloses the excavations of the **Templo Mayor**, the pyramid to the Aztec gods of rain and war Tlaloc and Huitzilopochtli. Streets and

This carved stone disk was excavated from the Templo Mayor. It represents the moon goddess Coyolxauhqui.

Pollution

Scratchy throat, watery eyes and a cough, cropping up soon after your arrival in Mexico City, are typical symptoms caused by nata *('scum'), the local term for air pollution. Don't worry – they'll go away once you move on. The capital has long had the unenviable reputation of being one of the world's smoggiest urban areas – and it is finally taking the problem seriously.*

Mexico City sits in a bowl, surrounded by mountains. More than half of the country's industry and more than a fifth of its population is located in the surrounding area. In winter, a temperature inversion causes thousands of tons of chemical particles from factory, incinerator and vehicle emissions, along with dust from the drained lake bed, to be trapped in the bowl's atmosphere.

Under the photochemical action of sunlight, the mix becomes a noxious brown smog. And because of the city's thin air at high altitude, fossil fuels burn inefficiently and produce more ozone than normal.

Birds have dropped dead out of the fouled sky here. The snowcapped volcanoes of Popocatéptl and Iztaccíhuatl disappear from view for months at a time. In January 1989, after schools had to be closed because of dangerously high pollution levels, the authorities began to clamp down on burning of refuse and dirty smokestacks.

Private cars are banned from the streets alternately, one working day per week. A 100,000-peso fine is imposed on violators. This has reduced pollution from car exhausts, but hasn't affected the smoke-spewing buses and trucks. And the rich got around the ban by buying a second car.

The most toxic winter in the city's history was in 1991 and it prompted President Salinas to take some radical measures in his antipollution campaign: he closed down the oil refinery at Azcapotzalco, which provided the major part of the city's gas and diesel fuel. This implied the laying off of some 5,000 workers at a cost of $500 million.

Early in 1992, the government created a commission to initiate corrective measures. These are to be financed within a $150 million programme. One proposal calls for introducing liquid-gas fuelled buses and trucks to replace those burning diesel oil and gasoline. These vehicles account for some 30 per cent of the city's smog.

Newspapers now give daily reports on the levels of carbon monoxide, sulphur, nitrogen oxide and other gases in the air and compares these with maximum levels for human health. All too often the levels are unacceptable; but the chronic situation has at least alarmed the government into action and the trend is toward improvement. As the chilangos *say, 'If you don't like the air, don't breathe it.'*

colonial structures covered the site until 1978 when work on a new metro uncovered a beautifully carved stone disk 3m (10ft) in diameter showing the moon goddess, Coyolxauhqui, with her head and limbs severed. According to legend, her brother Huitzilopochtli, the sun god, threw her from the top of a hill as punishment for rebellion. The find pinpointed the site of his great temple, for the disk of the dismembered goddess was placed at its base to re enact her fall and to represent the struggle between the sun and the moon. To give you an idea of its size, the pyramid was about 45m high (145ft); the cathedral towers make about 60m (200ft).

The ancient Mexicans always enlarged these monuments by building on top of the previous structure, removing nothing. Archaeologists uncovered seven layers of the Templo Mayor and a treasure trove of offerings to the gods underneath. These are displayed in the handsome **Museo del Templo Mayor**. The museum overlooks the site and is divided into sections representing the two temples which are set on a pyramidal base. It is open daily, except Mondays, from 9 a.m. to 6 p.m. The small entrance fee includes access to the excavations. The museum's bookshop has one of the best selections of foreign-language titles on Mexican art and antiquity.

The **Palacio Nacional** takes up the east side of the Zócalo. This is the seat of government, as indeed it was when the Palace of Moctezuma occupied the site. The Aztec emperor kept a collection of animals, water birds and fish here in what was the first zoo in the Americas. Cortés claimed the entire property and his son, Martín, sold it to Spain. The Spanish Viceroys lived in an earlier building. The present structure, begun in 1693, has undergone many changes, serving as a prison, army barracks and home of the first Mexican Congress. Maximilian enlarged it, and a third storey was added in 1927. The President's office is in an inner courtyard, though he usually works in his residence, 'Los Piños', in Chapultepec Park.

At 11 p.m. on 15 September, with the Zócalo packed with people, the President reads Father Hidalgo's declaration of independence, the 'Grito de Dolores', from the central balcony. Hanging above him is the liberty bell from Hidalgo's church, which rings in Mexico's National Holiday, answered by the great 12-tonne bell of the cathedral.

The central portal of the Palacio Nacional leads to a patio where a broad staircase ascends beneath **Diego Rivera's murals** of the history of Mexico. It's all here, with the whole cast of thousands spread out along three walls. It begins on the right, before the Conquest, with the blonde god Quetzalcóatl sailing across the sky and an upsidedown sun god bringing food and life to an Indian world. In the centre, violent battles engage the Spaniards with

Aztec eagle and jaguar knights. The Church burns Mayan books, but Bishop de las Casas protects the Indians, fending off a conquistador with his crucifix. The Inquisition strangles heretics in dunce caps. White-haired Father Hidalgo rallies the populace for independence. Benito Juárez holds the 1857 Constitution. American soldiers invade Veracruz and Emiliano Zapata proclaims 'Tierra y Libertad'. On the left, Karl Marx points to the future, while capitalists scheme and Diego Rivera's wife, the painter Frida Kahlo (she of the black eyebrows), represents education as the hope of the people.

Other Rivera panels depicting different indigenous tribes encircle the second floor arcade. In one, Malinche, her face hidden, walks behind Cortés, carrying their blue-eyed baby, symbolically the first *mestizo*.

Between the Palacio Nacional and the Supreme Court building to the south is the **Acequia Real**, once a canal, then a street, and now a likeness of the canal, with grass replacing water. The Zócalo's south side is occupied by the Federal District building and the old City Hall. On the east, the garden, restaurant and bar on the roof of the

The history of Mexico has resulted in a nation as rich and diverse as its people.

Hotel Majestic offer a terrific view of the whole plaza. Two blocks north, to the left of the Cathedral is the **Monte de Piedad**, the National Pawn Shop. There are always two long lines, people with objects to pawn or to reclaim. All around are rooms filled with an amazing collection of unclaimed stuff on sale. You just might find an attractive antique ring here amid the busts of Beethoven, old radios and musty sofas.

The Centro Histórico

The Zócalo is the heart of the *centro histórico,* old Mexico City. Its streets are studded with colonial palaces and churches, enchanting squares and many museums. The area behind the cathedral becomes a kind of market-cum-fair on weekends. You'll see a bird seller with his wares perched on his head, a honey vendor crushing combs of nectar into jars, a dancer in Aztec costume performing for a crowd. Hundreds of concoctions from medicinal plants are sold in an alley off C. República de Guatemala.

República de Brasil leads into the **Plaza de Santo Domingo**, one of the capital's most picturesque corners. Under the arcades public scribes type documents, fill out complicated

The 18th century Church of Santo Domingo: a marvel of Mexican baroque.

The Alameda Central, Mexico City's first park, home of the poplar trees (álamos) that gave it its name.

government forms or even compose love letters for illiterate or bashful clients. Here also are the printers who will make up a wedding invitation or business card on their hand presses.

Stop by the 18th-century Church of Santo Domingo to see the chapel on the right with a wall covered with ex-votos, small silver arms, legs, eyes and other bits of anatomy, offered in thanks for recovery from illness. (You'll see ex-votos and primitive paintings in churches all over Mexico.)

Take Calle Obregón from the square and turn left on Calle Argentina to the **Ministry of Public Education**. More than a hundred of Diego Rivera's earliest (1923) and best murals cover the walls of the courtyard, staircases and upper floors of the ministry. Look for the lively 'Day of the Dead' scene in the left rear of the patio. While Rivera was at work here, his contemporaries, **David Alfaro Siqueiros** and **José Clemente Orozco** were painting frescos in the **Colegio de San Idelfonso** around the corner. To compare the work of these three Mexican masters, follow Calle Argentina a block toward the Zócalo and turn left to No. 16 Calle Justo Sierra. Orozco's powerful and bitter scenes of injustice and war cover

Fabulous costumes and enthralling performances ensure the popularity of the Ballet Folklórico de Mexico.

walls on three floors of the inner patio. The Calle de la Moneda on the north flank of the Palacio Nacional is lined with vestiges of the viceregal period in *tezontle* stone. The first printing press in the western hemisphere was operating here in 1536. After the street becomes Calle Zapata it leads to Empress Carlotta's favourite church, **La Santisima**, with a Churrigueresque façade rivalling the Sagrario's.

Three blocks south of the Palacio Nacional on Avenida Pino Suárez, the **Mexico City Museum** is housed in the imposing colonial mansion of the Counts of Santiago Calimaya. Waterspouts in the form of cannons overhang the street. The museum is a good place to get your bearings – from its light and sound show, excellent topographical maps of the region, the lake and its Aztec dikes, models and engravings of the city at different stages of growth, and relics from every period.

Across the avenue an inscription marks the spot where Moctezuma first met Cortés. Behind it is the **Hospital de Jesús**, founded by Cortés and still functioning. The bust of the founder in the courtyard is one of very few memorials to Cortés in Mexico, where he is regarded as a perpetrator of genocide. Cortés died on a visit to Spain in 1547. His

If certain sounds capture the essence of a place, then the mariachis embody the spirit of Mexico.

remains were returned to Mexico for burial, but after independence had to be hidden. They were discovered in an urn in the wall of the hospital's church in the 1940s. A plaque to the left of the altar wastes no words on this remarkable man. It reads 'Hernán Cortés, 1485–1547.'

The Alameda District

The leafy island of the **Alameda Central** was Mexico City's first park, created in the late 16th century by draining a pond and planting the poplar trees (*álamos*), after which it is named. In the 18th and 19th centuries this was the centre of fashion, off-limits to the common people.

Today it is a favourite place for a Sunday family outing amid romantic statuary and fountains. Huge clusters of fancifully designed balloons bob along in the clutch of vendors, while children clamour for ice cream and lovers embrace on the benches. An orchestra plays in the Moorish bandstand on weekends. The scene is amusingly captured in Rivera's mural *A Dream of a Sunday Afternoon*

Garibaldi Square

Ay, Ay, Ay, Ay! If it's your birthday, (or anybody's you can think of) go to Garibaldi Square in the evening and ask the mariachis to play Las Mañanitas, *the lovely Mexican Happy Birthday song. Mariachis are musicians who play in groups, preferably including various sizes of guitar, a string bass and a trumpet or two. They wear the charro costume of short jacket, tight bell-bottomed trousers decorated with embroidery and silver buttons and perhaps a broad, embroidered sombrero. Originally the Mariachis came from Jalisco in Guadalajara, and they frequently play the song* Guadalajara *to prove it.*

Garibaldi Square is the gathering place for mariachis looking for work. They start drifting into the little plaza, six blocks north of the Bellas Artes building on Calle Lázaro Cárdenas, around 7 p.m. and will still be there until the early hours of the morning. Some mariachis stroll about here at any time of day. The square is one of the most cheerful spots in the city and when all the mariachis are playing to their various clients, it can get quite hilarious. Notice the statues of well-loved popular musicians around the plaza.

Many of the restaurant-bars cater to the 'Mexico by Night' tours, but these groups are outnumbered by Mexicans simply out for a good time or there to drown their sorrows to the accompaniment of appropriate music.

Adjoining the square is the **Mercado San Camelito**, *a block-long row of small kitchen-restaurants hardly more than two tables wide, each advertising more or less the same thing: pozole, birria, carne and pollo asado. It's all out in the open and smelling delicious, where tables with bowls of red and green salsa beckon and waiters hustle customers walking by. Some of the bars have the louvred swinging doors of old time cantinas and pulquerías. For a real taste and smell of the city, don't miss it.*

---

in the Alameda Park, created for the old Del Prado Hotel on Avenida Juárez. The hotel was wrecked by the 1985 earthquake, but the mural was spared and now has its home in the **Museo de la Alameda** at the western end of the park. The exhibit documents the fracas that erupted when the mural was unveiled and found to have the words *Dios no existe* ('There is no God') on a paper held by one of Rivera's sub-jects. After much controversy, the offending sentence was removed. Rivera himself appears as a pudgy boy holding the hand of a lady skeleton wrapped in a feathered serpent boa. Next door is the **Pinacoteca Virreinal**, exhibiting colonial period paintings in a former monastery. This is where heretics were burned at the stake during the Inquisition.

Across the Avenida Hidalgo, the park's northern border, the Hotel

Cortés occupies an 18th-century building that once provided lodgings to visiting monks. Its attractive patio is a good spot to rest your feet. The broad avenue covers the causeway on which the Spaniards fought their way out of Tenochtitlán on the *Noche Triste*. The **Iglesia de San Hipólito** on the far side where Hidalgo crosses the Reforma is dedicated to the Spaniards who fell in that battle. Look for the tablet carved in 1599 of an eagle carrying an Indian in its claws. Westward, between two facing churches sunk below the level of Hidalgo, the **Museo Franz Mayer** is beautifully installed in a former convent. Mayer, a German-born businessman, was a collector of all things Mexican: furniture, sculpture, church images, ceramics and curiosities, such as an exquisite mosaic composed of bits of bright feathers. There is a cafeteria and a peaceful patio where you can relax listening to classical music. The church to the right, **Santa Vera Cruz**, is so steeply tipped that the aisle goes uphill.

The **Palacio de Bellas Artes** (Fine Arts Palace) at the foot of the Alameda is a not-so-fine white marble Victorian pile typical of the grandiose projects of the dictator Porfirio Díaz. The interior, however, has a pure Art Deco rotunda and staircase of the 1920s leading to galleries where you can see murals all in one place by the Big Four of Mexican painting, Rivera, Siqueiros, Orozco and Tamayo. The ever-popular **Ballet Folklórico de México** has a programme of regional dances, staged here in a theatre famed for a Tiffany curtain made of thousands of glass beads depicting Popocatépetl and Iztaccíhuatl. Light played on the curtain recreates dawn and sunset on the mountains.

The Central Post Office is just across the Av. Lázaro Cárdenas from the Bellas Artes and just beyond it, on Calle Tacuba, is the **Museo Nacional de Arte**. The collection is heavy on 19th-century works, but there are interesting pieces from pre-Conquest times. The statue in front is **El Caballito**, (the Little Horse) whose pedestal gave the Zócalo its name. Coin collectors will enjoy the **Museo de la Numismática** on the first floor of the Banco de México building adjoining the Post Office. The Alameda's south side, Avenida Juárez, is an undistinguished commercial street. At No. 44, the **Museo de Artes e Industrias Populares** displays handicrafts from all over Mexico and operates a fixed-price shop. The marble monument across the way is the **Hemiciclo** dedicated to Benito Juárez.

Two of the city's liveliest handicraft markets are a ten-minute walk south of the Alameda. The **Mercado de Artesanías de San Juan** is on Calle Ayuntamiento, just off Calle López, Mexico City's Chinatown. Scores of little shops on two floors of this arcade sell the full range of Mexican crafts. The **Mercado de Artesanías de la Ciudadela** is five

Aerial view of the Glorieta de Insurgentes – the metro station Insurgentes in the Zona Rosa.

blocks down Calle Balderas on the Plaza de la Ciudadela. Here you can watch artisans weaving, painting and hammering away on their products. **La Ciudadela** on this square is a former arsenal, now the National Library.

Tourist guides joke that the **Torre Latinoamericana** at the end of the Alameda is 'the highest skyscraper in the world' – the first of its 42 floors is 2,415m (7,925ft) above sea level. The top floor bar and restaurant is a good place to watch the sun go down and the lights of the city wink on. A monastery founded in 1525 as headquarters of the Franciscan Order once stood here, but it was destroyed in the 19th-century Reform and the sunken **Church of San Francisco** behind the tower is all that's left. A Methodist chapel occupies the cloister.

Across Calle Madero is a Mexico City landmark – the **Casa de los Azulejos**, covered entirely in 18th-century blue tiles from Puebla. It was built in 1596 for the Count of Valle de Orizaba. The Sanborns restaurant chain converted the elegant inner court into a restaurant where homesick Yankees flock to get a solid breakfast and hamburgers. You'll be served under a balcony where the suitor of the daughter of Valle de Orizaba was hanged after murdering the Count on the staircase. Down the street at No. 17, the **Palacio de Iturbide**, where the general was proclaimed Emperor of Mexico in

53

1822, is now a bank. The three-storey courtyard is a beauty, often used for art exhibitions.

Before leaving this part of the city, riding enthusiasts may want to check out the hand-tooled, silver-mounted saddles at the **Museo de la Charrería**, the horsemen's museum, three blocks west of the Pino Suárez metro station, on Calle Izagaza.

The Reforma and Zona Rosa

The **Paseo de la Reforma** is one of the world's great boulevards, conceived on a grand scale by Emperor Maximilian and still able to handle traffic without losing its majestic ambience. The Reforma proper is the straight stretch between the Alameda and Chapultepec Park, though additions continue from both ends. Maximilian intended it to link his residence in Chapultepec Castle with the seat of government in the Palacio Nacional. This grand scheme was to be called the 'Avenue of Illustrious Men', lined with statues of same. Porfirio Díaz completed the central section and unveiled the first of the statues, very few qualifying as illustrious today, but handy for the pigeons.

Roundabouts called *glorietas* interrupt the avenue and serve as reference points for direction. The first, heading southwest from the Alameda, is **Colón**, the monument to Christopher Columbus; next comes **Cuauhtémoc**, the last Aztec ruler shaking his spear defiantly; then the multi-coloured glass pillars of a fountain illuminated at night; then **Independencia**, better known as **El Angel** for the winged victory atop its column; at the entrance to the park, **Diana**, armed with her bow, graces a fountain.

One block to the right of Colón, on Calle Ramírez, the **Monumento a la Revolución** looms over the Plaza de la República. Which revolution? The one of 1910. It paved the way for the modern state and is generally what is meant by 'the Revolution' The arched cube and dome, part of a legislature building never completed, was salvaged to become the shrine where Pancho Villa and other heroes are buried. Locomotive 67, planted on a platform, commemorates the role of railroad men in the fighting. The **Frontón México**, the capital's main centre for gambling on the Basque court game, *jai-alai*, is across the street.

To the right of Cuauhtémoc, where Insurgentes crosses the Reforma, Calle Sullivan leads to the **Jardín del Arte**. On Sundays the garden blooms with paintings that artists display for sale. To the left of the avenue is the worldly enclave of the **Zona Rosa** where streets are named after cities. You might not recognize Amberes as Antwerp or Niza as Nice, but if you need help, this district has policemen whose badges identify the languages they speak. Pedestrian zones with

Chapultepec Park and its myriad colours create a carnival atmosphere that reaches its peak on Sundays.

sidewalk cafés go on for several blocks, with a number of attractive boutiques, silver shops, restaurants and nightclubs. The Mexico City Tourist Office at Calles Londres and Amberes operates **Infotur**, a phone-in service (525-9380) in English and Spanish with current schedules of events and performances.

There's a wonderfully cluttered labyrinth of handicraft and food stalls in the **Mercado Insurgentes** between Londres and Liverpool just off Florencia, and a government-owned FONART fixed-price shop upstairs at Londres 136. The concentration of tourist trade has tarnished the Zona Rosa's pretensions to elegance. The fancy shops have moved with the money to the **Polanco District**, on the right flank of Chapultepec Park,

where the newest highrise luxury hotels are clustered.

When cars stop for the traffic lights on the Reforma they are pounced on by agile windshield-washing boys. One intersection becomes a stage for jugglers and acrobats, another is the nighttime turf of a kid who takes a mouthful of petrol from a can and blows out a plume of fire, then runs to collect pesos from drivers. Here and there you may spot one of the few remaining Victorian mansions that once lined the avenue. Now they are in the shadow of some

of the hemisphere's most arresting modern office buildings. Look for the new **Bolsa**, the Stock Exchange, an angular sandwich of two-tone glass layers beside a multifaceted beehive of mirrored panels.

Chapultepec Park

The 'lungs of the city', wooded **Chapultepec Park** spreads over 400 hectares (988 acres). It was a royal retreat for the Aztec kings, who are believed to have planted some of the venerable *ahuehuete* trees (a kind of tall cypress) surrounding the hill at the park entrance. They also built an aqueduct to serve Tenochtitlán that ran down what is now Chapultepec Avenue.

Chapultepec means 'Grasshopper Hill' in Náhuatl. The hill has often played a central role in the city's history. Cortés fortified it, the Spanish viceroys built their residence on its summit and it was a military academy when the US troops of General Winfield Scott stormed the heights in 1847. The monument of six white columns at the base of the hill commemorates **Los Niños Héroes**, the 'boy heroes', cadets who fell in the battle.

Renovated, the **Castillo de Chapultepec** became the palace of Maximilian and Carlotta and then the

The winged victory of Independencia, better known as El Angel, on the Paseo de la Reforma.

residence of a number of Mexican Presidents. It has been the **Museo Nacional de Historia** since 1944. On the ground floor, portraits of leaders and summaries of their political fortunes may end up confusing even the most earnest history student. All the players in the pageant of Mexican history are assembled in a mural by **Juan O'Gorman**. Upstairs, David Alfaro Siqueiros does a masterful job of cramming a historical epic on nine walls of two rooms. In one, a senile Porfirio Díaz sits with his foot on the laws; in another Emiliano Zapata reins in his galloping horse just short of the door.

Another ingenious, more easily comprehensible telling of the Mexico story awaits you in the **Caracol**, a snail-shaped glass museum tucked into the hillside, down from the castle entrance. Entering at the top, you descend a spiral corridor lined with small historical dioramas from viceregal days onward. There is a collection of remarkable photos of the 1910 Revolution. The last turning brings you to a dramatic rotunda of carved stone where the Mexican flag and a sculpture of the eagle and serpent emblem are lit by a shaft of sunlight.

After all this walking around, you may be ready to sink into a comfortable chair at the nearby **Audiorama**, a peaceful garden enclosure where you can close your eyes and relax to a free recorded classical music programme.

The Aztec Calendar of Stone (above) and a Mayan mask from Palenque (right) are both on display at the Museo Nacional de Antropología.

Chapultepec Park was once the preserve of the rich and privileged; now it truly belongs to the people. On Sundays you'll think all of Mexico City's millions have turned out to picnic on the grass, play ball with the children, row boats on the lakes and climb on a wooden horse to pose in a Pancho Villa sombrero for a park photographer. The shady walks are lined with food and drink stalls, balloon sellers, and artists painting clown make-up on children's faces.

The **Zoo** here is famous for its four giant pandas. Three were bred and born in the zoo, a most unusual occurence. The noisiest inmates, howler monkeys from the Yucatán jungles, outroar the lions.

The President's residence is at the southern end, where an expressway divides the park. On the far side, an amusement park boasts dozens of rides, including a monster roller-coaster called the *montaña rusa*, or Russian mountain, that proves very popular. The park and rides are free from 9.30 a.m. to 1 p.m. on Sundays.

Nearby, the indefatigable Diego Rivera embellished the city water-works with a grotesque mosaic sculpture-fountain of the rain god, Tlaloc, spread-eagled in a basin and spurting water from every pore.

The Museum of Anthropology

The **Museo Nacional de Antropología** is not only by far the world's greatest collection of early Meso-American art, it is also a brilliant, unforgettable architectural masterpiece. A visit to this treasure house in Chapultepec Park would alone make the trip to Mexico City memorable. The architect, **Pedro Ramírez Vazquez**, also designed the Templo Mayor Museum, the Caracol Museum, Azteca Stadium, the Basilica of Guadalupe and many other Mexico City landmarks. Here he has used local stone and ancient motifs to create a most original modern setting that subtly evokes the past.

Guarding the entrance is a 4th-century BC, 167-tonne statue of Tlaloc, God of Rain. (When it was moved from its original location across the valley in the 1960s, thunder, lightning and a downpour broke over the city.) The museum is built around four sides of a court 82m (268ft) long open to the sky, reminiscent of the ceremonial spaces in pre-Conquest ruins. Overhanging the entrance to the court is an immense aluminum roof that seems to float without support,

Beautiful ornate headdresses are worn on 12 December, when celebrations mark the day of Our Lady of Guadalupe, patron saint of Mexico.

with sky visible on all sides. This canopy is pierced by a massive column that disappears through a hole. Perpetual 'rain' showers from this opening, forming a curtain around the column and the figures in relief that cover it. Unseen above, a steel mast projecting from the column holds the roof up by cables. The court radiates power, mystery and serenity.

A good introduction to the museum is given in a small amphitheatre beneath the reception hall. In a 20-minute multimedia show, the history of ancient Mexico is traced, from the killing of a mastodon (you'll keep hearing his trumpeting as you walk around the museum) to the arrival of the Spaniards. There is a special orientation room for children, too, and an excellent shop. You'll have to pay a small charge to take your camera inside.

The exhibition halls begin on the right with an explanation of the science of anthropology, emphasizing that 'all cultures are equally valuable'. Succeeding rooms deal with the origins of the earlier settlers and the pre-classic period up to about 700 BC, throughout the Meso-American region – the area inhabited by the advanced cultures, roughly from the lower half of Mexico through the Mayan sites in Guatemala, Belize, Honduras and El Salvador. The rooms are then devoted to specific groups and sites, the Teotihuacán pyramid-builders,

The Basilica of the Virgin of Guadalupe.

the Toltecs with one of their characteristic warrior-shaped temple columns, and in the great central hall, the Mexica, or Aztecs.

The Aztec hall is dominated by the huge, intricately carved Calendar Stone, discovered in 1790 under the Zócalo. In its centre is the sun. Symbols represent the 18 months of 20 days, plus five 'unlucky' days, of the Aztec year. Rosettes mark the 52-year intervals initiating a new cycle, when temples were rebuilt or dedicated. A particularly frightening statue of the earth goddess Coatlicue, with a serpent head and necklace of severed hands and heart is offset by a poetic representation of Xochipilli, lord of music and dancing, seated with legs crossed and face uplifted. Look for Moctezuma's iridescent feather headdress, a copy of the original sent by Cortés to Charles V.

Next comes the Oaxaca room, with the Mixtec breastplate of gold, silver and turquoise and a reproduction of a Monte Albán tomb. The Gulf of Mexico room is noteworthy for its Olmec sculpture. Look for the outstanding small figure of a bearded man known as 'El Luchador', the wrestler. Here are beautifully carved jade objects from the ritual ball game called *yugos* (yokes) and *hachas* (axes), the immense helmeted Olmec heads and a superb Huastec figure of a youth with his body 'tattooed' by bas-reliefs.

The Maya room is equally fine. Among its many treasures are small terracotta figurines from Jaina near Campeche showing the costumes of

Maya personages in minute detail; two magnificent portrait busts from Palenque; and stone stelae bearing reliefs of ceremonial scenes and Mayan hieroglyphics from Yaxchilan in the Chiapas rainforest. The remaining hall is dedicated to the appealing primitive art of northern and western Mexico.

Immediately above these halls, the upstairs museum illustrates the daily life of the descendants of each of these ancient peoples, or at least of the Indian communities now living in the same areas – Mayas above Mayas, Zapotecs and Mixtecs above the Oaxaca hall, and so on. It is best to begin above the entrance and work around the courtyard anticlockwise, for the first room offers an introduction to the materials and methods of ethnology, the study of races. The costumes and handicrafts of each tribe and photographs of their present-day environments are exhibited with life-size models of family groups. The best view of the court and the suspended roof is from the gallery above the Mexica hall.

The courtyard arrangement makes it easy to step outside at any point and find a bench for a little rest. Here you can read on the walls Spanish translations of Aztec poetry, surprisingly sensitive for a warrior race. There is a pleasant restaurant on the garden level. Ideally, however, you shouldn't try to take in the whole museum in one visit. As in virtually all Mexican museums, explanations are only in Spanish. A modest fee is charged for guided tours in other languages. Check at the ticket counter.

Two other collections close to the entrance to the Reforma as it enters Chapultepec Park are worth a visit if you are not pressed for time. The **Museo de Arte Moderno** exhibits Mexican painting and sculpture from the turn of the century to the present. The **Museo Rufino Tamayo** is less a place to view this painter's work than another example of Mexican creativity in architecture. It includes Tamayo's collection of contemporary art from other countries. Tamayo, the last of the great Mexican muralists, died of pneumonia in June 1991.

Other Points of Interest

The **Plaza de las Tres Culturas**'s significance is summed up in its name – Plaza of the Three Cultures. It is near the northeastern end of the Reforma in what was the important Aztec market town of Tlateloclo. The ruins of a temple pyramid are overlooked by the colonial church of San Francisco and the modern glass and steel Ministry of Foreign Affairs – hence, the three cultures. The final battle of the conquest was fought here and a plaque movingly records the event: 'On 13 August 1521, heroically defended by Cuauhtémoc, Tlatelolco fell into the hands of Hernán Cortés. It was neither a triumph nor a defeat: it was the painful birth of the *mestizo*

> ### Quake!
>
> *At 7.19 a.m. on 19 September 1985, when millions of people were on their way to work or getting ready for the day, a major earthquake rocked Mexico City. For three minutes (an eternity in earthquake time) buildings swayed, cracked and crumbled. Rippling streets tossed cars, and electricity, telephone, gas and water lines were broken. A cloud of dust rose over the city, rent by explosions and livid with the glow of fires.*
>
> *It was the worst quake in the city's recorded history: 8.1 on the Richter scale. Some 10,000 persons died, 855 buildings were badly damaged or destroyed (including the 25 buildings of the National Medical Center and General Hospital), and 70,000 were left homeless.*
>
> *The outpouring of international assistance was immediate, but years after the quake many victims were still living in temporary shelters and tents around the city. And it will be many more years before some of the damaged hotels and office buildings in the Alameda District and elsewhere downtown are repaired or rebuilt. The new hotels are constructed to be earthquake-proof. Towers above 18 floors fared better than lower buildings: the Torre Latinoamericana skyscraper swayed, but stood firm.*
>
> *Mexico's volcanic and earthquake-prone character is caused by the collision of plates of the earth's crust off the Pacific Coast. The Continental plate, 'floating' on a layer of molten rock a hundred kilometres or so down, slides westward, while the Cocos plate grinds beneath it in a northeasterly direction. When the plates get stuck, pressure builds up that is released in tremors. Most are brief and barely noticeable, but understandably nerve-racking, and Mexicans will brace themselves in doorways during these shocks on the theory that these will hold even if the ceilings fall.*

nation that is Mexico today' The apartment houses nearby were badly damaged by the earthquake that rocked Mexico City in 1985.

Continuing out the Calzada de Guadalupe 4km (2.5 miles) brings you to one of the world's great religious shrines and the centre of Catholic Mexico, the **Basilica of the Virgin of Guadalupe**. Ten years after the Conquest, a newly baptised Indian named Juan Diego had a vision of the Virgin. She re-

quested that a church be built in her honour on this site, where an Aztec temple to the mother of the gods had been razed by the Spaniards. The bishop was suspicious of Juan Diego's tale. The Virgin again appeared to the Indian, instructing him to pick roses and take them to the bishop. Roses miraculously appeared on the dry hillside and Juan Diego wrapped them in his cloak. But when he took them to the doubting prelate, instead of roses, the cloak had Mary's image im-

printed upon it. Convinced by this miracle, the bishop ordered the church built to display the cloak. The present Basilica is the fifth to hold this relic – visitors can view it close up from an underpass beside the altar without disturbing the mass.

Extravagant costumes shimmer in the light and music and dances erupt in honour of Mexico's patron saint.

The modern shrine can hold 20,000 faithful under its high ceiling of pine timbers contributed by Canada. Earlier churches stand nearby on the **Plaza de las Américas**.

Our Lady of Guadalupe has become the patron saint of Mexico and her day is 12 December, with feasting, rejoicing and pilgrimages. Copies of her image are omnipresent throughout the country and it's a common sight to see pilgrims on their way to the shrine carrying her banner. You are almost certain to see worshippers fulfilling a vow by approaching the church on their knees. Even the most sophisticated Mexican is likely to keep a small replica of the Virgin at home. (The *colectivo* minibuses marked 'Villa' on the Reforma end their run at the Basilica and the Metro Line 6 station 'Villa' is nearby.)

Mexico City's flea market is the **Mercado de la Lagunilla** just east of the intersection of the Reforma with Calle Lázaro Cárdenas at the roundabout marked by the statue of José Martí. Everything imaginable is sold here, probably even fleas. Some

Corrida

The art of bullfighting inspires extremes: some see it as unacceptably cruel animal torture, while others esteem it as a richly symbolic drama involving the courage Ernest Hemingway called 'grace under pressure'. The corrida, or running of the bulls, is not really a fight, for the outcome – the death of the bull – is predestined, regardless of what happens to the men who confront the beast.

The corrida follows a fixed pattern and is divided into three parts, or tercios. The opening procession begins with the mounted alguaciles, who come before the presiding official to receive the key to the gate where the bull awaits; all participants parade to music and salute the President.

The first tercio begins when the gate is banged open and the bull charges out into the ring. The fans watch carefully to see if he has the size, speed and fury required of a toro bravo. The matador's assistant capemen are first into the ring, taunting the animal with their capes so the matador can assess the bull's strength and behaviour – how the bull hooks with his horns, how quickly he turns and any other helpful clues.

When the matador himself enters, he incites the bull to charge his cape. If the matador is both skilful and has a single-minded bull, he will keep it charging, while he performs graceful capework close to the horns. When the crowd is pleased, it will cry 'Olé!' in rhythm to the passes.

After the capework, in the second tercio, the matador or one of his assistants will place banderillas (steel barbs on decorated sticks) into the hump of the bull's neck muscle. He calls to the bull, offering his body as target; when the bull charges, the torero plants the banderillas on the run.

Weakening the bull's neck muscle is the job of the mounted picador, or spearman, who is the 'heavy' of the corrida. When the bull charges his horse (protected by thick padding), the picador jabs the neck with a lance, the pic. The bull's readiness to keep charging, despite the pic, is considered a measure of its bravery.

In the final fatal tercio, the matador exchanges his cape for the muleta, a red cloth draped over a sword; he attempts to demonstrate his control and his courage with a series of passes. Among the many traditional passes, certain require the matador to plant his feet together and take the bull's charge stiff as a statue, drawing the beast safely past with the muleta. In others, he will pull the animal's charges in a close circle around him. His jacket may be red with the bull's blood, or ripped by a horn tip. And this is where he is very likely to be gored, as most matadors eventually are.

If the bull is a brave one, returning to the charge with determination, and if the matador is at the *same time courageous, graceful and working close to the horns, the crowd may demand music and the 'Olés!' may rock the bullring. More often though, the critical Mexican aficionados will whistle and hoot at any flaw in the performance.*

The end comes when the matador goes to the barrera, *takes another sword, and salutes his lady-love or whoever else he may dedicate the bull to. After a few more passes, he will 'fix' the bull so that its head is down and its eyes focused on the* muleta. *This exposes the point on the spinal vertebrae where the matador aims his sword. To kill properly, he must plunge in over the horns. If all goes well, the bull will drop dead on the spot.*

If the matador has performed well, the presiding official may award him the bull's ear, two ears, or – triumph! – two ears and the tail. If the bull has been particularly brave, he will be applauded, too, and on rare occasions is awarded the honour of being dragged around the ring. More often, hooting and bottle-throwing fans show that they think it's the matador who deserves this particular treatment.

Seating in all corridas *is less expensive on the* sol *(sunny) side than on the* sombra *(shady), a tradition inherited from Spain. In Mexico City sunny seats can be more comfortable in winter. And this is where you'll find the crowd at its liveliest.*

of the junk is so obviously worthless, one speculates whether it might be staged to make the buyer pounce on a 'find' when spotting an apparent antique amongst the trash. This is the place to practise your bargaining technique and to spend an entertaining Sunday morning. It is open the rest of the week as well.

On the other side of town, follow Insurgentes Sur to the **Insurgentes Metro Station**. This sunken circle shows how a necessary facility can be turned into a community asset. The plaza has shops, restaurants, book fairs, art exhibits and sometimes concerts. Further south on the right at Calle Filadelfia, an explosion of colour announces the Polyforum Siqueiros, a crown-shaped arts centre covered by David Alfaro Siqueiros's violent images. Inside, an auditorium houses the artist's immense three dimensional mural, *The March of Humanity Toward the Cosmos*, which you view from a moving platform. The 12-sided structure contains a theatre, café, exhibition galleries, and a collection of works by the artist.

To the right of the next roundabout is the **Plaza México** – at 50,000 seats the world's largest bullring. The season, from November to April, is the off-season in Spain, so the world's top matadors are seen here. At other times of the year apprentice bullfighters (*novilleros*) take over to fight younger, smaller bulls (*novillos*) and the Sunday afternoon card is billed as a

67

This fresco, by David Alfaro Siqueiros, adorns the walls of the Autonomous National University of Mexico.

Novillada instead of a *Corrida de Toros*. The posters look the same, so be alert for the wording. Novilladas can be thrilling – after all, every matador has passed this way – but they can be quite dismal, too. At least the tickets are cheaper.

Many travel agencies include a bullfight in their Mexico City tours, which is a convenient way to get a ticket – you'll have a good seat along with transportation to and from the ring. (Cabs are hard to find around the Plaza México after a bull-fight.) Farther down, still on the right, look for Diego Rivera's mosaic

on the **Teatro de los Insurgentes**. Even here, Rivera is preaching politics.

Insurgentes next crosses the suburb of San Angel (see p71) and enters the **Pedregal**, a vast sheet of lava more than 3m (10ft) thick, now covered by a residential district and the **Ciudad Universitaria**, the campus of the Autonomous National University of Mexico.

The lava flowed from a small volcano around 450 BC when the site was already inhabited. While quarrying building stone here at the turn of the century, engineers discovered skeletons and artifacts dated back to

The Charreadas – a type of rodeo – attracts a huge following.

A truly Mexican produce – maize – is on sale at this market stall.

1100 BC. Some of these may be seen in tunnels in the lava at the **Copilco Archeological Site**, off the avenue to the left.

The university was founded in 1551 and is the oldest in the Americas, while its campus is one of the most modern. The Ciudad Universitaria complex, opened in 1954, shows why contemporary Mexican architecture has admirers worldwide. The ten-storey block on stilts encrusted with mosaics is the **Central Library**, designed by artist **Juan O'Gorman**. Murals and mosaics decorate almost every building.

One of the most striking is the three-dimensional Siqueiros mural on the **Rectory**, designed to be observed from cars moving along Insurgentes. Rivera's contribution is on the other side of the avenue, stone reliefs of Mexican sports from past and present on the **Olympic Stadium**.

There's one more sight to see on Insurgentes. The eruption that buried Copilco also covered Mexico's oldest complete pyramid, the round pyramid of **Cuicuilco** where the avenue crosses the Periférico. The structure – three concentric rings of baked clay and stone – had apparently been abandoned for centuries before being swallowed up by lava. A small museum displays objects found on the site and explains the origins of the Pedregal.

AROUND THE CAPITAL

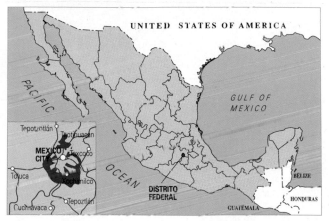

SAN ANGEL AND COYOACÁN

San Angel was once a village surrounded by orchards that the viceroys and elite of colonial Mexico favoured for their country houses. The metropolis has grown around and beyond it, leaving San Angel a village within the city, an island of narrow, cobblestone, up-and-down streets, attractive villas behind high walls and luxury boutiques. *Colectivos* to San Angel run regularly from the Chapultepec metro station. They – or your cab – can drop you off on Insurgentes Sur across the avenue from the **El Carmen** church and convent. The

rooms of the convent are furnished with colonial antiques. Note the lovely tile washbasins. (Less enchanting are the mummified nuns and priests exposed in the crypt.)

From the convent it is a short walk up to the Plaza de San Jacinto. At No. 23, there is a memorial tablet to Captain John O'Reilly and 70 ill-advised Irish members of the US Army's St Patrick Battalion who deserted General Scott's forces in 1847 to fight for Mexico. They were captured and hanged in this square. Among the Sheehans and Kellys note the unexpected name of one Herman Schmidt.

San Angel is most fun to visit on a Saturday morning when the **Bazar**

71

Relax in this luxurious restaurant in San Angel, or sample the lively Sunday 'river walk' in Xochimilco.

Sábado on the Plaza de San Jacinto and a nearby *tianguis* (street market) are in full swing. The Bazaar, open only on Saturday, is a collection of superior handicraft, jewellery and dress shops tucked into corners around the courtyard of an old house. A buffet lunch is served in the patio, where musicians and fountains play. A pleasant walk up shady lanes brings you to the **San Angel Inn**, probably the only restaurant in the world with its own chapel. It occupies the main building and gardens of a historic hacienda. (You can go in for a look without dining.) Across the streeet is the former home of Diego Rivera, now the **Diego Rivera Studio Museum**. It contains a clutter of the papier mâché skeletons and dolls that fascinated the prolific Mexican artist.

Farther out, **Coyoacán** (Place of Coyotes in Náhuatl) is more accessible and less manicured than San Angel. It has the atmosphere of an artist's colony – there are bookshops serving coffee, sidewalk cafés, a fanciful bandstand in the zócalo that looks like a carousel without the horses, and a number of interesting crafts shops near the 1583 church of San Juan Bautista. Cortés lived here while the unhealthy ruins of Tenochtitlán were being cleared of the dead and debris following its fall. His first wife died in the old **Casa de la Malinche** on Calle Higuera soon after her arrival from Cuba. Cortés was rumoured to have murdered her in order to be with his Indian mistress.

A few blocks from the centre, you'll find the **Frida Kahlo Museum** behind a blue wall at Calle Londres 247, in the house that Diego Rivera shared on and off with the painter Frida Kahlo, his wife. Her introspective canvases and self-portraits are full of the suffering she endured after a crippling accident. You'll recognize her face in many of Rivera's murals. It's an interesting, idiosyncratic museum. Look for her

73

'Place of the Flowers', Xochimilco

In Aztec times flowers, trees and vegetables were planted on artificial rafts of mud and reeds set afloat in Lake Texcoco. In time, these chinampas *became anchored as roots reached the lake bottom. Indian market gardeners ferried their produce in canoes to sell on the canals of Tenochtitlán. The 'Floating Gardens of Xochimilco' have blossomed into a Mexican Venice. On flower-bedecked barges, boatmen pole festive groups or romantic couples through tree-lined waterways. Mariachi musicians on the docks board the barges or cruise the canals on boats of their own, coming alongside to play requests. Photographers implore passengers to immortalize the moment by posing beneath the floral arch with the barge's name – 'Conchita' and 'Lupita' seem to be favourites.*

Time and growth have not been kind to Xochimilco. The whole town is still devoted to gardening and there is a marvellous flower market in the centre, where you can buy carved, painted canes and fresh fruit as well. But the canals are green with pollution, and the bottleneck of taxis and buses around the plaza on Sundays seems to have taken root like the chinampas. *It is not a tourist trap, however – most of the crowd is Mexican, many in family groups with picnics, and the music, hurly-burly and general commotion are authentic. All tour companies include Xochimilco, which is 25km (15 miles) from Mexico City centre. It can also be reached in about an hour by a combination of Metro line 2 to Taxqueña and* colectivo *No. 36 from the station, for a roundtrip cost of one dollar.*

Facing the zócalo is the Franciscan church and convent of San Bernardino, founded in 1535. In the park there is a monument to Martín de la Cruz, an Indian who wrote a catalogue of medicinal plants used by the Aztecs, and to Juan Badiano, another Indian at the convent, who translated it into Latin and made it a standard reference work.

collection of primitive ex-voto paintings – one illustrates the escape of a grateful man who was cut down after being hanged. (The museum is open from 10 a.m. to 2 p.m. and 3 p.m. to 5 p.m., closed Mondays.) Nearby at Calle Viena 45 is the fortified house of **Leon Trotsky**, now a museum where his books, piles of clippings and a Russian typewriter are preserved just as he left them. The precautions of this outcast Communist were unavailing; an agent of Stalin split Trotsky's skull with an ice axe in 1940. He is buried in the garden. It is open for visits from 10.30 a.m. to 2 p.m. and 3 to 5 p.m. Tuesday through Friday, and from 10.30 a.m. to 4 p.m. on weekends.

Diego Rivera's personal collection of pre-Conquest art is the

Anahuacalli, a black lava pseudo-temple designed by the artist on the outskirts of Coyoacán. It is best visited by taxi or tour bus, for other transportation is scarce. Among the treasures here are comical clay figurines with rings in their large noses from the west coast Nayarit people and a wonderfully alert, striped terracotta Colima dog once placed in a tomb to guide his dead master to the underworld. This museum opens at 10 a.m. closes between 2 and 3 p.m. and reopens until 6 p.m. It is closed Mondays.

THE PYRAMIDS

'Awesome' is the word to describe **Teotihuacán** and its pyramids. The city was built on a superhuman scale two thousand years ago by an unknown race, and had been in ruins for more than 600 years when the Aztecs rediscovered it and called it 'the place where men became gods'. No one knows what the Teotihuacán people called themselves. This was the first great city of the western hemisphere, with a population of more than 100,000 and an area of 11sq km (7sq miles). Its style and symbols were copied by the Toltecs and Aztecs who succeeded them in the central highlands. The city was a place of pilgrimage and trade, as testified by objects from all over Mexico found in its ruins. But it had no fortifications and presumably never recovered from an attack by barbarians who sacked and burned it

around AD 700. By the 16th century it had become so covered by earth and vegetation that the Spaniards marched past without even seeing it.

Teotihuacán is just over an hour's drive north of Mexico City. At the entrance a small museum provides an introduction to the site. It opens on to the 39m-wide (130ft) **Street of the Dead**, the broad esplanade that ran 4km (2.5 miles) from the Pyramid of the Moon at the north end to a still unexcavated point to the south. Straight ahead at the avenue's midpoint is the **Ciudadela** (citadel), a walled quadrangle with the **Temple of Quetzalcóatl**, the feathered serpent, at the rear along with a dozen ceremonial platforms on four sides. A small pyramid covers in part the earlier temple to the god which you can enter from the right. A staircase is flanked by heads of the serpent, whose body wriggles along the base. Framed heads of the white-fanged deity alternating with that of the round-eyed rain god Tlaloc and conch shell designs cover the walls.

The Street of the Dead is lined with stone temple foundations, all formed by a sloping skirt (*talud*) surmounted by a boxed mural panel (*tablero*), the characteristic elements of Teotihuacán architecture. In the time of the Aztecs, these monuments were earth-covered mounds thought to be tombs – hence the street's misleading name. It is, in fact, the grand aisle of an open-air cathedral, big enough to accommo-

The awesome Pyramid of the Sun of Teotihuacán, seen from the Pyramid of the Moon.

date the scores of thousands who thronged here on sacred days.

The **Pyramid of the Sun** on the right served as the altar, rising 64.5m (215ft) on a base 221m (738ft) to the side. Stand at the foot of the stairs and imagine the wonderment of the crowds looking up to the priests at the summit chanting to trumpets and drums. The sheer mass of the pyramid is overwhelming. It is composed of an estimated 3.5 million tonnes of mud brick and stone, raised around AD 100 by a workforce of thousands without the benefit of metal tools,

draught animals or the wheel. Originally, the pyramid and most of the other monuments of Teotihuacán were covered with a thick layer of plaster. You can see from bits here and there that much of it was painted red. In this and other reconstructed archaeological sites, the restored sections are indicated by a regular peppering of small stones in the cement. The 247 steps to the top are easier going up than coming down, when the steep pitch gives some people vertigo. Persistent sellers of flutes and 'genuine' clay idols stake out the places where climbers stop to rest. But the effort is rewarded by a sweeping view of the orderly plan and grandeur of Teotihuacán. Behind the pyramid and south of the Citadel are the geometrical grassy

The Feathered Serpent

*Ancient Mexicans ranked their gods in terms of local needs: where crops depended on uncertain rainfall, the rain god was supreme; where sunshine was unreliable, the sun god took precedence. **Quetzalcóatl**, the Feathered Serpent and God of the Morning Star, the Wind and the Arts, was different. He was a more universal deity, perhaps introduced by the people of Teotihuacán and exalted by the Toltecs. According to legend, he created man with his own blood, then turned himself into an ant in order to steal a grain of maize from the ants. He gave this most important life-sustaining gift to men. And Quetzalcóatl did not require human sacrifices.*

*Around 968 a Toltec king named Ce Acatl Topiltzín also served as a priest of Quetzalcóatl in Tollan (Tula). He was fair-skinned and had a beard, which is unusual among the Indian race. Topiltzín was a peaceful ruler, but he fell afoul of a war-like brother and was forced to leave Tollan. To the confusion of scholars, this genuine historical figure entered legend as a demi-god, also called Quetzalcóatl. It is told that he moved east, as far as the land of the Maya. The Maya venerated him as **Kukulcán**, meaning 'feathered serpent' in their tongue. And it is obvious from many features of Chichén Itzá and other cities, that Toltec influence was present at about that time.*

Topiltzín-Quetzalcóatl-Kukulcán moved on. He is said to have sailed toward the east on a serpent raft, promising to return. And so, four centuries later, when Moctezuma learned that bearded men sailing on 'floating houses' had arrived in his dominions he was sure the god had kept his promise. He greeted Cortés as the returning deity, welcomed the Spanish forces into his capital and opened the way to the Conquest.

lumps that outline miles of still unexcavated sections of the city. On the summit platform a wood and thatch temple originally stood. The pyramid was built on top of a 300 BC shrine and cave, which were worshipped as the birthplace of the sun.

The **Pyramid of the Moon** stands in its own plaza at the end of the ceremonial avenue. From the sides and rear you can see how these ruins looked before excavation was undertaken at the turn of this century. The moon pyramid is 45m (152ft)

high but because it is built on a rise, its summit is roughly even with the Pyramid of the Sun's. A number of palatial residences of priests or nobles have been discovered nearby. The **Palace of Quetzalpapálotl** to the west has two elegant courtyards reached by a stair surmounted by a giant serpent's head. Carved reliefs on the columns of the lower patio represent a bird, the *quetzal*, and a butterfly, whose Náhuatl name, *papálotl*, is curiously like the French *papillon* and Italian *papavero*. Discs of obsidian filled the now-vacant eye holes and traces of red, green and blue colouring can be seen. The whole city must have glowed.

Teotihuacán is remarkable for ts well-preserved murals. Hands holding jaguars in nets are on the walls of the **Jaguar Palace**, and underneath the bird-butterfly house the older **Temple of Feathered Shells** is decorated with parrots and conches. The most lively and extensive paintings are in the **Tepantitla** complex near the parking lot behind the Pyramid of the Sun. In one scene, swimmers frolic in a lake. Another shows ball players with blue bats. Pre-Colombian field hockey?

Returning to Mexico City, make the short detour to **Acolman** to see the early Augustinian monastery, now a museum. Whenever you see a major church out in the middle of nowhere, you can bet that it was the site of an important Aztec temple. The monks first destroyed the heathen shrine, then replaced it with their own. This one is a good example of a church-fortress, built when the Indians were still considered a threat. It has medieval crenellations on the roof and a strong protective wall around the buildings. The cells and cloister still reflect the austerity of monastic life.

PUEBLA

The trip to Puebla makes a memorable day's outing. The highway climbs to 3,000m (10,000ft) through

---

The Bug Lives!
More than a dozen years after the last Volkswagen 'Beetle' rolled off the company's production lines in Germany, a VW factory in Puebla is turning out some 450 a day. Priced below $6,500, the Beetle is Mexico's cheapest and most popular car.

The US, Japanese and European car models circulating in Mexico are all produced nationally under licence. Volkswagen has been manufacturing Beetles here since 1964. An estimated 42 per cent of Mexico City's taxis and some 400,000 of the capital's cars are Beetles, called simply 'sedans'. The basic design is pre-World War II. Since 1991, all new cars must be equipped with catalytic converters to reduce pollution.

---

pines and upland meadows and descends through apple orchards where drivers stop to buy cider. Closer to Puebla, kids line the road to sell sweet potato candy. Along the way, you get a great close-up view of Popocatépetl and Iztaccíhuatl from the rear. The entire city is a national historical monument, noted for the tiles that decorate its every dome, façade and colonial mansion.

The elaborate church of Tonantzintla, on the outskirts of Puebla, is well worth the detour.

PUEBLA

The cathedral, Mexico's second largest, overlooks a shady zócalo lined with shops and cafés under arcades. To its rear on Avenida 5 Oriente, the **Palafox Library** in the former archbishop's palace contains interesting maps and manuscipts amid baroque panelling.

Across the zócalo, two blocks down the pedestrian Calle 5 de Mayo, the church of **Santo Domingo's Rosary Chapel** is Mexican Churrigueresque at its most brilliant. Every centimetre of this 17th-century jewel-box masterpiece is worked in gold-covered wood and plaster set off by a white stucco background. Wildly ornate carvings of cherubs and saints are lost in the foliage of a gold jungle. The main altar of the church is equally fine, with 18 polychrome portraits of saints ensconced among gilt columns. The buff, white and gold geometrical panels of the nave frame doleful virgins and angels, while inlaid lapis lazuli, onyx, and blue and white Puebla tile embellish the pulpit and walls.

Puebla was built as a new city replacing the Toltec centre at Cholula nearby. Its narrow streets are lined by houses with overhanging balconies and walls typically patterned by brick cross-hatching studded with blue tiles. Here and there a bell tower or church dome rises above the roof line, its zig-zag tile designs gleaming yellow, white and blue in the sun. The **Parián Market** is good for onyx, embroidery and ceramics. The

adjoining artists' quarter has cobblestone streets where studios and workshops invite browsing.

Guides always take you to the **Convent of Santa María** on Avenida 18 Poniente, the 'hidden convent'. It operated clandestinely from 1857 to 1934 after being closed by the Reform laws. Entry was through a concealed door in an adjoining house that led to two small cloisters and an upstairs gallery, where the nuns could peek into a church below. Policemen in the stationhouse next door must have been in on the secret – or singularly un-

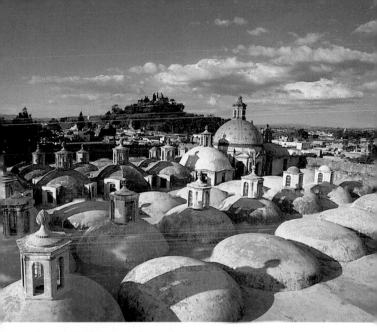

observant. The most interesting room is the kitchen. It has a circular tile stove of delicate blue and white stars and flowers. If you take a meal in Puebla, sample the local speciality, turkey with *molé poblano* sauce – created by nuns, it is composed of 24 spices and bitter chocolate.

The domes of Puebla are best seen from **Los Fuertes** on the hill overlooking the town. A monument commemorates the 5 May 1862 defeat of 6,000 French soldiers by 2,000 Mexicans, which delayed the French capture of Mexico City and installation of Maximilian as emperor.

A detail from the church of Tonantzintla (left) and (right) the colonial church of Cholula.

Village churches in the state of Puebla are painted bright colours and inlaid with patterned brick and tile. Two of the most photogenic are just outside **Cholula**, on the outskirts of the city: **Tonantzintla** and **San Francisco de Acatepec**. The Pyramid of Cholula was as big or bigger than the Pyramid of the Sun at Teotihuacán. What you see today,

81

The pyramids of Tula and its famous carved stone giants.

covered with grass and trees is an inner pyramid, exposed when the Spaniards removed the face of the great shrine. It was surrounded by hundreds of smaller pyramids, according to Cortés. On his march to Tenochtitlán he forestalled an ambush here by slaughtering thousands of the population and burning the temples. These were later covered by churches – there was supposed to be one for every day of the year. This may once have been true, but now

82

TULA AND TEPOTZOTLÁN

The capital of the Toltecs, Tula, is about 85km (50 miles) north of Mexico City on the toll road 57D. Visits to the site should include a stop at **Tepotzotlán**'s famous baroque church. **San Francisco Javier** was completed for the Jesuits in 1762, only five years before the order was expelled from Mexico. The façade and campanile are as delicately and deeply carved as any in Mexico, but it is the interior that will bowl you over. Its low, domed vaults in white set off six amazingly complex chapel *retablos*, carved wood altar screens covered with gold leaf. Each of these is populated with a host of angels, cherubs, saints, martyrs, shells, curling leaves, inset paintings and statues, windows, columns, obelisks and medallions curving up toward the ceiling. It outdoes anything else of its kind on an order of ten to one and cannot fail to impress even the most hardened sightseer. The adjoining monastery buildings have been converted to house the **Museo Nacional del Virreinato** (National Museum of the Viceregency). The site comprises a small village founded around 1600. The museum houses a collection of religious art, open from 11 a.m. to 6 p.m., except Mondays.

Tula, the ancient Tollan, has a special place in the art and religions of Mexico. The city was built by the Toltecs, a tribe from the north that arrived in central Mexico around

there are 47, which is quite enough for a town of 20,000. One is on top of the pyramid, and from this summit you can get an idea of the extent of the ancient city. You can also creep through tunnels below made by archaeologists and see the skeleton of a sacrificial victim beneath an altar in the diggings.

725, round about the time of the fall of Teotihuacán. They preserved and spread many of the traditions of the Teotihuacán people, only adding new features of their own. Tollan, 'the place of the reeds', was their capital until it was overthrown and destroyed by the Chichimecs, perhaps an advance guard of the Aztecs, in 1168.

Its centrepiece is the three-stepped **Pyramid of the Morning Star**, one of the forms of the feathered serpent god, Quetzalcóatl. The roof of a temple on the platform was once upheld by the four Atlantides, 4.5m (15ft) pillars in the form of warriors. Each holds arrows in the right hand and a sling in the left. The staring sockets were filled with white stone eyes. Each wears a feather headdress and ear ornaments. The statues were originally painted red and on the chest of each is the butterfly symbol of life also seen at Teotihuacán; on their backs are shields in the form of the sun, adorned with human heads. Note their leggings and sandals.

Square pillars to the rear, decorated by warriors with an eagle headdress, also supported the roof; the fallen round columns in front framed a doorway.

An Indian from Chiapas wearing a traditional hat. (Chiapas Indians are in fact the direct descendants of the peoples who lived here before the Spanish Conquest.)

Around the rear base of the temple, a bas-relief depicts a procession of jaguars and coyotes, each with a collar suggesting mastery by man, and eagles or vultures eating human hearts. The face of a monster with a human head emerging from its mouth is a representation of Quetzalcóatl as the Morning Star arising from the darkness.

Tula has two ball courts and a typical Toltec portico of dozens of columns between the Pyramid of the Morning Star and the Pyramid of the Sun on its left. On the right is the **Coatepantli**, a wall decorated with rattlesnakes devouring men that leads to the **Palacio Quemado**, the Burned Palace, also filled with columns around open patios.

An excellent little museum illustrates the history of Tula and the Toltecs. Note the wide-hipped terracotta fertility dolls (pre Toltec) found in the region. They are very much like images found in prehistoric sites in Asia and the Middle East. Mesoamericans (the prehistoric settlers of Mexico) discovered agriculture, the first step toward settled civilization, about 2,000 years later than the peoples of the Middle East and in complete isolation from the rest of the world. Even so, their accomplishments in art, architecture and calculation compare favourably with any other ancient civilization. Who knows how they might have developed if their culture had been allowed to progress undiscovered and uninterrupted?

TO THE COAST

CUERNAVACA

Over the mountains south of Mexico City, **Cuernavaca** luxuriates in a setting drenched in colour. Blossoming flame trees, bougainvillaea, hibiscus, camelias and poinsettia blaze along streets where jacarandas stand in blue pools of fallen petals. The rich and famous long ago picked the city for their winter homes because of the year-round spring climate – their red-roofed villas are hidden behind high walls. More recently, the 90-minute drive to Cuernavaca has become such a favourite outing from the capital that on major holidays the toll expressway, Highway 95, is often converted to one-way traffic to handle returning crowds. (A parallel, prettier non-toll road remains open in both directions.) This is also the route to Taxco (pronounced *Tahss-co*) and Acapulco, respectively three hours and six hours from Mexico City.

The road from the capital climbs through pine woods and meadows, then drops to 1,666m (5,000ft) where

Cuernavaca looks out over the lush Morelos Valley and back at the snow-capped volcanoes. Everything as far as the eye can see was once part of the 65,000 square-kilometre domain granted to Cortés when he was given the title Marquis del Valle de Oaxaca by King Charles V. After tearing down an Aztec pyramid temple for stone, the old campaigner built a fortress-palace for himself around 1530. He introduced sheep, cattle, the silkworm and Cuban sugar cane, still extensively grown in the valley. The palace is now the **Museo de Cuauhnáhuac** – the Aztec name for the town ('place at the edge of the forest') distorted by the Spaniards to Cuernavaca ('cow's horn'). There are cultural and historical exhibits, including relics of the original inhabitants. A highlight of the museum is a Diego Rivera mural of the valley's history commissioned in 1928 by US Ambassador Dwight Morrow as a gift to Mexico. It depicts the conquerors lolling in hammocks while natives tote sugar cane, and repeats the often-painted scene of Spaniards burning Cuauhtémoc's feet in the vain attempt to force him to reveal the location of Moctezuma's treasure. **Emiliano Zapata** appears on his white horse.

Morelos was the base for his peasant rebellion and the museum features Zapata relics, including superb photos of the revolution. One shows the hacienda where Zapata was invited for lunch, then murdered by an 'honour guard' in 1919. 'Better to die on your feet than live on your knees,' he always said.

The **Cathedral** is set back from the bustle of the streets in a park-like corner. The crenellations on the roof proclaim it to be from the early 16th century, when churches doubled as strongholds. The interior is a surprise – under the old barrel vault, the altar is an abstract modern construction, lit by sunbeams from high windows. Unconventional, too, is the rousing 'Mariachi mass' on Sunday. In refurbishing the nave in 1967, 17th century frescoes were uncovered showing the martyrdom of St Felipe de Jesús, crucified in 1597 in Nagasaki with 25 Franciscan missionaries. Across a courtyard, the **Capilla de la Tercera Orden**'s baroque façade has the added charm of naïve Indian dancing-men designs, a reminder of the Indian labour that built these churches. The altar's *retablo*, the gilded carved wooden screen, is notable. A band of blue Puebla tile around the walls enhances this attractive chapel.

A short walk up the Avenida Morelos leads to the **Jardines Borda**. The city has let the 18th-century formal gardens become overgrown, dark and drooping. They are no longer the showplace of yore. Something similar might be said of Cuernavaca as a whole – industrial development clouds the once-clear air, traffic clogs the downtown streets and the three connected plazas of the zócalo with their side-walk cafés are a crowded bazaar. Woolworth heiress Barbara Hutton's home has become a Japanese restaurant. The old street market has been moved across the ravine that divides the city, a short walk behind and to the left of the Palace of Cortés. Although confined to a large enclosure, the market is nevertheless bursting with vitality and overflowing with exotic produce, including an assortment of powders, leaves, bottled snakes, bark and roots guaranteed to cure everything from phlebitis to impotency. More of the same may be examined in the **Museo de Medicina Tradicional** at 200 Calle Matamoros in a house called la Casa del Olvido ('House of Forgetfulness'), said to have been used by Maximilian for trysts with his Mexican mistress.

A short taxi ride will bring you to the **Pyramid of Teopanzolco**, still within the city. From its top you can look down on to an earlier pyramid inside, covered by the outer structure. Until 1910 the mound was thought to be a hill, but when Zapata put some guns here and their recoil dug into the thin topsoil, the building stone beneath was revealed.

Cuernavaca is most enjoyable if you have time to stay a few days. In the environs are some fine restaurants, two golf clubs, haciendas and mansions turned into hotels. There are worthwhile short excursions to the attractive village of **Tepotzlán** and the archaeologically important hilltop ruins of **Xochicalco** dating from 200 BC.

TAXCO

The drive to **Taxco** takes about an hour and a half, part on the highway to the coast and part on a pleasant winding road. About 20km (13 miles) before reaching Taxco, a turn-off to Toluca on the right marked 'Grutas' leads to the **Grutas de Cacahuamilpa**, one of the most extensive cave systems in Mexico. Huge caverns 60m (200ft) high drip with stalactites and amazing limestone formations that run some 70km (45 miles) undergound, most still unexplored. Guided tours are from 10 a.m. to 3 p.m., to 4 p.m. on Sundays, and take about an hour and a half.

The white walls, red roofs and flower-filled balconies of Taxco spill down a green hillside. The blue and yellow dome and twin pink spires of **Santa Prisca Church** provide the centrepiece of this picture postcard scene, a long-time favourite with tourists. The whole town is a national monument. It was founded by Cortés to exploit Indian silver mines, but the richest desposits were discovered in the 18th century by José de la Borda. He became so

The white walls and red roofs of Taxco greet you as you approach the town. Right: the wildly ornate church of Taxco.

wealthy that he built gardens and mansions and paid for the total reconstruction of Santa Prisca, explaining that 'God has given to Borda, now Borda gives to God.' The church's rosy façade fairly writhes with spiral columns and twisted martyrs. Faces peer out of the stone at every angle. The ornate golden altar is worthy of this community of jewellers. You'll find their shops in every street and especially around the Plaza Borda, the sloping zócalo in front of the church.

Mines that honeycomb the hill beneath the town are still being worked – you'll hear the steam whistle when shifts change – but today the source of wealth is silver jewellery. An American, William Spratling, started it all when he came to Taxco in the 1930s, set up a silver workshop and taught local craftsmen to use ancient designs in modern products. The **Museo Guillermo Spratling** (open Tuesday through Saturday, 10 a.m. to 5 p.m.), just below the square, holds the American's fine collection of pre-Columbian art and features historical exhibits as well.

The fun in Taxco is to climb up and down the narrow streets, comparing prices and bargaining, watching artisans cutting, filing and polishing silver, obsidian and semi-precious stones. Take a break on a restaurant balcony overlooking the square. Descend the long stairs lined with market stalls and food stands where you are served from steaming clay cauldrons. On John F. Kennedy street at the bottom, cabs and *colectivos* pass continually to take you back up the hill. From the heights of Monte Taxco, reached by overhead cable cars, there's a great view over the town and a nine-hole golf course. Find a seat at sunset on one of the hotel terraces on the slopes overlooking Taxco, and watch the sky turn pink behind Santa Prisca and the lights of the town spark like fireflies.

ACAPULCO

After Taxco, the road drops 900m and as you wind through the river valleys and canyons of the Sierra, the climate changes to tropical. The pot of gold at the end of this rainbow route is **Acapulco**, the ultimate resort. Arriving from Taxco or the airport, you come upon it after topping a ridge. There below is a sweeping bay, with white ships on blue water, a long curving beach lined with high-rise hotels and the city cradled in the arm of green hills.

Acapulco is probably the best known city in Mexico, after the capital. Its modern fame was launched as the kind of place for which the phrase 'jet set' was invented, the winter playground of the pampered. One of the first luxury hotels boasted a private swimming pool for every bungalow guest and free pink-striped jeeps from room to beach. Soon the publicity that follows the glamorous attracted the rest of us –

Beaches stretch for miles in the bay of Acapulco – the ultimate resort.

upwards of 3 million guests a year (including Mexican tourists). Fortunately, Acapulco is big enough and organized enough to keep everyone happy, and it's still growing.

There are some 20 beaches in the Acapulco area. The main strip in front of the big hotels facing the bay is about 11km (7 miles) long and so broad that it is never really crowded. But often it seems there are more wandering vendors of straw hats, T-shirts, hammocks, dresses, jewellery, handicrafts, kites and toys, food and drink, than there are swimmers. There's a strong undertow at times: watch the notice of swimming conditions posted at hotels.

Once the big beach was considered a series of beaches, still identified by bus stop signs along the six-lane main drag, **La Costera Miguel Alemán**. Now they have more or less merged into one. La Condesa, the 'afternoon beach', is in the centre of the bay and at the heart of the action. To its left is Icacos Beach and the navy base with its three-masted training ship; to the right are Morro, Hornitos and Hornos Beaches and the harbour for yachts and deep-sea fishing boats. Hornos has restaurants and changing rooms, but no hotels, being reserved as a park for the public. (Actually, all beaches in Mexico are public.) Beyond, the promontory of the **Península de las Playas**

closes the bay. Its beaches, Caleta, Caletilla and Angosta, are the 'morning beaches' in coves with no surf. Launches from Caleta run regularly the short distance to **La Roqueta** island where the swimming and diving is good from several beaches connected by paths through the woods. Older, smaller hotels and clusters of ageing villas mark this peninsula as the original centre of a less-pressured Acapulco tourism in the 1930s.

Farther on are the cliffs of **La Quebrada**, world renowned for the divers who plunge from its heights into a narrow inlet.

From La Quebrada it's a short walk downhill to Acapulco's non-touristy zócalo area. The square is so overhung with trees, it's cool and almost dark at midday. It's backed by an Art Deco cathedral that began life as a cinema. Cafés flank two sides. You can buy a paper, have a coffee and people-watch people who aren't just more people-watchers. For a moment you might forget this is swinging Acapulco, but at night you'll be aware that a busy red-light district is nearby. In back of the zócalo, along Avenida Cuauhtémoc, it's the working world of shops and dentists and bus stations for the million citizens who aren't on holiday.

La Quebrada: famous for its dare-devil divers.

It is entirely possible to spend all your time in Acapulco in your hotel without being bored. The big hotels have pools with the swim-up bars invented here, tennis courts, water skiing and para-sailing off the beach, more or less continuous entertainment – from beach and pool sports to Mexican music and dance festivals – and there'll be plenty of shopping on the premises. A choice of in-house restaurants will serve Mexican or international cuisine. Transportation is offered free to and from the harbour for sunset cruises, swimming and dancing cruises, open bar 'booze cruises', glass-bottomed boat cruises; you can be taken to a golf course, the bullfight (on Sundays), *jai-alai* arena or a round of discos. When you're too sunburned or tired to leave your room, you can watch balloonists and para-sailers cross the sky and speedboats send up spray, then see the sun go down in a burst of crimson and gold. Lift the phone and a tray of margaritas will be on its way. The hotels near the airport and the big surf Revolcadero Beach are self-contained resorts.

In town there are plenty of comfortable hotels with none of these extras, but very reasonable prices. They are found on the inland side of the Costera Miguel Alemán. Just walk across the boulevard to swim. You can hop in a horse-drawn, balloon-draped *calandria* and clip-clop along to the Condesa Beach area's boutiques and the bars that have 'Happy Hour Now!' displayed at all

93

hours. There are even stockbroker's offices for those who refuse to get away from it all.

If the market tumbles, don't worry. For next to nothing you can board one of the fuming, roaring buses and ride for miles along the coast, perhaps beyond the naval station and over the ridge to **Puerto Marqués**. Here steep hillsides enclose a small bay and a beach solidly packed with open-air restaurants favoured by the locals. The single street of Puerto Marqués has wandering pigs the way other towns have dogs. It could be a million miles from the sophisticated luxury just over the rise. In the opposite direction from the centre, a half hour past La Quebrada, your bus or cab will reach **Pie de la Cuesta** beach, where the mangrove-lined **Laguna de Coyuca** on the other side of the highway was the location for parts of the *Rambo* movies. Bird-watchers might enjoy a 'jungle cruise' on the launches waiting here. If you go in late afternoon, slide into a hammock on the beach and be prepared for one of the sunset spectaculars for which this spot is famous.

It's after sundown that life begins for many in Acapulco – night clubs, discos, Mexican folklore, fiestas and stage shows (for some reason,

transvestite acts are a favourite in several). The choice is so wide that you couldn't exhaust the possibilities in a month. An excellent variety show with or without dinner is staged nightly except Sunday from 8 to 10.30 p.m. at the **Centro Internacional de Acapulco** convention centre behind Icacos beach. Big name artists perform at the major

The sun sets over the bay, but Acapulco will cater for its guests late into the night.

hotels in winter. Many of the night spots and restaurants are up on the hills where you can relish a harbour view along with the lobster. Along the Costera, hamburger stands and ice-cream parlours are open all night long. So are the Indian women, seated on the sidewalk with their wares, while their children sleep beside them, wrapped in *serapes*.

The present tourist boom, which began in earnest in 1955 with the opening of the superhighway to Mexico City by President Alemán, is the second golden age of Acapulco. The first was in the 17th and 18th centuries, when the port was a busy link in the trade between Spain's Asian possession, the Philippines, and the mother country, via Mexico.

Only Way To Go

Wherever there's a road in Mexico, there's a bus. The bus is the country's favourite mode of travel – very cheap, comfortable and a good way to see both the scenery and the people. First-class buses usually really are first class, with air-conditioning and a bathroom; second class can be okay, but probably uncomfortably crowded. The two services usually operate from different stations. Head for the Central de Autobuses (or Camiones) de Primera Clase.

Directo doesn't always live up to its name. Especially on the outskirts of town, the bus driver will often stop to let people on or off. A lot of eating goes on during long bus rides. You may be offered a snack or a drink, and your neighbour will be pleased at your offer to share your own provisions. It's a good way to break the ice and strike up a conversation.

Many buses have a red light over the driver's seat. It is supposed to blink when the bus exceeds 90km/h (55mph). Not to worry – it probably doesn't work anyway. Buses also have a cut-out that bypasses the muffler, supposedly giving the engine more power. Drivers are supposed to use the muffler in town, but don't.

Many drivers have a motto over their seat. A favourite that may give you second thoughts: 'If this is my last trip, God, may it lead to you.'

Acapulco's great bay was discovered in 1523 by one of Cortés's lieutenants sailing in a ship carried in pieces by Indians across the Tehuantepec Isthmus. Later, galleons displacing 1,000 tonnes called the 'Nao de China' sailed to Acapulco from Manila, bringing porcelain, silks and ivory.

To defend this treasure against pirates, the **Fuerte de San Diego** was built in 1617. Today the fort is a museum that traces the early history of the city. It was destroyed in an earthquake in 1776, but soon after it was rebuilt, Mexican independence put a stop to the Asian trade. The last 'Nao de China' arrived in 1815. Then

Acapulco dozed off for over a hundred years until it was discovered by tourists. The fort is between the yacht harbour and the zócalo. It is open daily except Mondays from 11 a.m. to 5 p.m.

Acapulco may not be a fishing village anymore, but they're still fishing. Deep-sea sport fishing craft leave from the harbour in the morning. Take a look at who's catching what when they return around 1 p.m. and if you like what you see, negotiate a deal. Prices range from about $100–300 for a boat holding four or five fishermen. There's an international sailfish tournament here in April. Watch the pelicans swarm

Puerto Marqués – a far cry from its sophisticated neighbour, Acapulco, but a popular spot nevertheless

when nets are pulled in on Las Hamacas beach near the yacht basin. There's a water-ski ballet and stunt show at 9 p.m. off this beach.

For children there's the **Papagayo Park** amusement rides, open at 4 p.m.; and at the **Centro Internacional de Convivencia Infantil** (CICI) there's a pool with waves and a giant slide, a dolphin show and lots to do. Big kids can try surfing in the real waves at Revolcadero Beach, but the breakers are whoppers.

OAXACA AND CHIAPAS

For the traveller who wants to experience rugged, remote country with authentic Indian flavour, the southern states of **Chiapas** and **Oaxaca** offer all this along with impressive ruins and spectacular scenery. This is an area of varied climate and geography, agricultural and artisanal rather than industrial. When you get tired of the highlands you can descend into tropical rainforest or go surfing from one of the beaches along the Pacific coast.

OAXACA

Oaxaca (pronounced *wa-ha-ka*), the state that seems to have everything – from sandy shoreline and handicrafts to ruins and history – is at last coming into its own. Over much of its past, Oaxaca was hard to get to, cut off by mountains from Mexico City and the main travel routes. Now that access is easy (it's only 40 minutes away from the capital by air) visitors are finding it hard to leave.

Oaxaca the city will slow down your clock. The pressure is off the minute you settle into a chair at one of the cafés bordering the central gathering place, the zócalo. There's plenty to do, but why rush? Now's the time to enjoy a *café con leche* or a *cerveza*, and have your shoes shined while you watch the world go by. Across the way is the birdcage bandstand, and if it's evening, there may be garlands of coloured lights shining in the trees and you'll soon be treated to *marimba* music or old-fashioned waltzes by the municipal band.

Streets around the plaza and adjoining cathedral are for people, closed to cars. The balloon seller will float past, kids playing tag will dart and squeal around the fountains, an Indian woman with a thick pigtail will hold up for your appraisal a belt she has woven, and the rich aroma of sizzling food from a sidewalk stall will perk up your appetite. Time to amble over to a restaurant and leave sightseeing for *mañana*.

There are no big modern buildings in Oaxaca. As a national monument, construction is strictly controlled. The administrative halls and mansions of colonial times are low, sober structures of greenish stone with iron grilles on the windows and arches leading into patios centred around a well. The largest downtown

A young girl from Juchitán, Oaxaca.

hotel is a converted 16th-century convent. This leaves the skyline to the belltowers of stately churches, the most beautiful being **Santo Domingo**, set back on a terrace of roses and hibiscus. Begun in 1575, it was rebuilt with walls 2m (6ft) thick after being destroyed by an earthquake. More destruction was to come: although Oaxaca was the birthplace of Benito Juárez (the Zapotec Indian who studied for the priesthood and became President in 1861, instituting La Reforma), the laws of Juárez closed the churches. Santo Domingo and its monastery was a barracks and stable from 1860 to 1900.

Much of the interior is a brilliant restoration. The barrel vault and walls are encrusted with ornamental gilt stucco and paintings, made more dazzling by a white plaster background and black outlining. Saint Dominic stands in the centre of the golden three-tiered main altar screen.

The sumptuous Rosary Chapel to the right attracts the most devotees. A magical moment may envelop the church when an Indian woman, kneeling in a shaft of light from the stained glass windows, spontaneously lifts her voice in a hymn. The ceiling just inside the entrance is covered by a multi-branched grape vine with moustachioed grandees and queenly dames representing the genealogy of St Dominic. It culminates not in the saint, but in a Virgin and child, added during restoration.

The Museo Regional de Oaxaca occupies a cloister attached to the church. Oaxaca is perhaps the most 'Indian' state of Mexico. Half the population speaks Zapotec or Mixtec dialects as their first language. The museum's ground floor is devoted to the costumes, handicrafts and festivals of these tribes. The upper galleries belong to their ancestors, the builders of Monte Albán, the sacred city on a mountaintop that overlooks Oaxaca.

The relics of three main phases of the city's existence are on display: Monte Albán I (500–100 BC), II (100 BC–AD 350) and III (350–AD 750). In room 2, the Mixtec treasures of Tomb 7 are the museum's great prize. More than 500 pieces of jewellery and artifacts were found in this tomb in 1932. Here is the famous gold burial mask and breastplate, a necklace of gold turtles, huge pearls, jewellery of coral, amber and jade, cups of rock crystal and a skull partly covered in turquoise mosaic. There are skulls showing traces of operations on the brain – but no indication whether the patient survived.

The Mixtecs had mastered the art of moulding gold by the 'lost wax' method. The form was first carved in clay, then covered with wax and overlaid again by clay. The wax was melted and drained and the cavity filled with molten gold. Then the clay was removed and the gold image polished to perfection. In another room you'll find some of the glass beads the conquistadors traded to

Judging by the range of food on display, the Benito Juárez Market, in Oaxaca, is probably the best in the country.

the Indians for gold. If they had found Tomb 7, they would have melted the treasure into ingots, as they did with most Indian gold. The museum is open from 10 a.m. to 6 p.m., Tuesday through Friday and from 10 a.m. to 5 p.m. on weekends.

Another marvellous collection is in the **Museo Rufino Tamayo** on Calle Morelos. The painter, a native son who died in his 90s in 1991, converted a colonial house and patio and filled it with his superb selection of ancient Mexican art from every period and civilization. Look for the charming little Olmec 'sunbathers' in room 1, the clay model of a ball game with spectators and a great helmeted Nayarit warrior in room 2, and in room 3, two amazing terracotta figures, an old man 'chewing herbs' and an enthroned figure of the skeletal God of Death, among the many masterpieces. This museum is open from 10 a.m. to 4 p.m., closed Monday and Tuesday.

Valley Villages

Each village in the valley of Oaxaca has its own market day, wisely scheduled not to conflict with others, and each has its special product.

The Sunday market in **Tlacolula** is one of the best. On the way, stop at the **Tule Tree** (above), an ancient ahuehuete cypress, an incredible 60m (164ft) in circumference. A short detour to **Teotitlán del Valle** brings you to the valley's most famous weaving centre. Along the road you'll see fields of maguey, the spiked leaf agave grown here to make **mezcal**, a local tequila. You can visit a distillery to see it done and to sample the product. Tlacolula merchants will show you how to drink it straight, with a special reddish salt that has powdered maguey worms in it. Some bottles come with a guisano (worm) inside to prove it's the real thing.

The Friday market in **Ocotlán** is not very touristy, and the Thursday market in **Zaachila** even less so, but they couldn't be more picturesque. The market women don't particularly like having cameras stuck in their faces – this is where a telephoto lens is in order. See the many varieties of fresh and dried chile peppers, watch how each fruit is polished and piled artistically, notice how the mangoes are carved like pine cones and the crisp white jícamas, a crunchy, juicy tuber tasting like a semi-sweet radish, are neatly sliced for nibbling. You'll see women wearing the very shawls, blouses and red and black skirts sold in Oaxaca's craft shops. Alas, beware of pickpockets and bag-slashers in the crowds. **San Bartolo Coyotepec** on the road to Ocotlán is where the velvety black pottery comes from. Stop at any of the houses with pots outside to see them being made.

The **Basílica de la Soledad** two blocks farther on honours the city's patron saint and is the focus of more or less continual festivities. There's a small market of food stalls and curios, including little ex-votos in fake

A spiky landscape in Teotitlán del Valle, where fields of maguey punctuate the valley.

silver, limbs, hearts and lungs and animals. Dancing takes place on the broad plaza in front. The much-reconstructed **Cathedral** near the zócalo is always crowded. Sometimes you may hear *marimba* music inside when a wedding is underway. A block down Calle Independencia from the Cathedral, the **Teatro Macedonia de Alcalá** has been restored to its 19th-century gold and velvet glory, a perfect little Victorian opera house.

The markets of Oaxaca and neighbouring villages would be sufficient reason for your visit. Indian *tianguis*, or street markets, are all over town and women and children offer their wares wherever you turn. Unusually fine handicraft shops occupy the interiors and patios of colonial mansions. But the daily action is in the covered **Benito Juárez Market** behind the zócalo and on Saturday in the sprawling **Mercado de Abastos** west of the *Periférico* ring road. Both are places where the populace comes for supplies. Each section has its own cloud of scents: sweet, fermented, spicy, floral, bakery, fishy, and so on. And each has stalls heaped with the freshest, most colourful produce. You'll find straw hats and baskets, embroidered blouses, rugs, shawls and sandals in the covered market. The quality may not be as high as in the craft shops, but they're authentic, and Oaxacans buy them too. Bargaining is part of every transaction. Early on Saturday, Indians from the countryside come into the Abastos Market with chickens and pigs, hand-made brooms and sacks of charcoal. When they've done their business, they fill up with *enchiladas* wrapped in banana leaves at the numerous food counters.

A unique feature of Mitla are these 'friezes' called grecas.

YAGUL AND MITLA RUINS

Trips to the village markets can be combined with visits to some of Mexico's most interesting ruins. The Tlacolula road continues to **Yagul** and Mitla. Most tours sail right past Yagul, but it's well worth the short detour, if only for the view. From the crumbled fortress, with its cactus sentinels, you look down on a roofless labyrinth, the **Palace of the Six Patios**, a ball court and the full sweep of the valley. Perhaps because it is usually empty of visitors, Yagul may seem like your own discovery.

Mitla comes next, about 40km (25 miles) out of Oaxaca. The ruins are right in the village. These palaces and courtyards of 15th-century Mixtec design were inhabited at the time of the Conquest and most were used, rather than destroyed, by the Spaniards, which explains their excellent state of preservation. The exception was the temple, as usual now covered by a church. The palaces are unlike anything you'll see elsewhere. They are covered by panels of projecting mosaic composed of little limestone bricks tightly fitted without cement. The concept is unique and the work that went into it immense. Because some of the designs resemble the scrollwork of Greek friezes, they are called *grecas*. The massive stone lintels and pillars of the **Group of the Columns** were somehow dragged from a quarry 20km (12.5 miles) away. In the second courtyard two tombs can be visited. In the Tomb of the Cross, girls wrap their arms around a central pillar, and by measuring the gap between their hands, calculate the number of years to their marriage.

Across the road, the **Church Group** of three patios shows that the mosaics were originally painted white on a red background. Mitla is a Zapotec town today and the local guides will claim the palace-builders were of their tribe. Who can blame them? In the town centre, the **Frissell Museum**, open from 9 a.m. to 6 p.m., exhibits Zapotec figurines found in the valley by American archaeologists based here. There's a shop and pleasant restaurant attached.

MONTE ALBÁN

Monte Albán, atop a high ridge 8km (5 miles) west of Oaxaca, is an astonishing sacred Zapotec city that for more than 1,200 years embodied the grandeur of one of ancient Mexico's most important civilizations. The site itself, a narrow plateau falling off steeply on all sides into valleys, is quite extraordinary. Around 500 BC the mountain crest was levelled by enormous effort to create a ceremonial plaza 300m long and 200m wide (980ft by 650ft) for temples, a ball court (*juego de pelota*), an observatory and palaces for the priest-rulers. In AD 700 all this was abandoned, though the surrounding hillside was later used as a burial ground (where Tomb 7 and other Mixtec treasures have been unearthed). Apparently the ancient city was closed to all but priests and nobles. The remains of the houses and terraced fields of the peasantry who supported them covered the mountain, where many unexcavated mounds are visible.

Lifted into the open sky, Monte Albán seems designed as a meeting place of men and gods. One can easily imagine how dazzling the plaza must have been when its monumental structures were covered with plaster and painted red and white. The pyramidal platforms originally held temples and palaces of wood. If you're on a tour or engage a guide, you'll probably begin by circling the ruins from behind in order to visit Tomb 104. Burials were usually beneath the floors of houses. Descending steps into this one, a flashlight is needed to see the head of a rain god and some faded frescoes over the entrance to the crypt. Then a path through the underbrush emerges on to the **North Platform**, overlooking a sunken patio (*patio hundido*) and the whole complex. To the right, a massive platform covers an earlier building. Again a flashlight is needed to enter a narrow passage and see the original carved façade inside.

The next structure shelters the **Danzantes**, slabs carved soon after

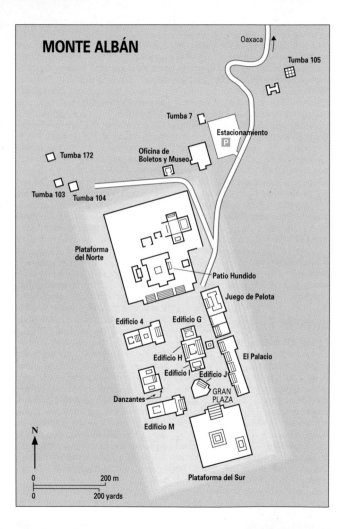

MONTE ALBÁN

Oaxaca

Tumba 105

Tumba 7

Estacionamiento

P

Oficina de
Boletos y Museo

Tumba 172

Tumba 103   Tumba 104

Plataforma
del Norte

Patio Hundido

Juego de Pelota

Edificio 4   Edificio G

Edificio H   El Palacio

Edificio I

Edificio J

Danzantes   GRAN
                      PLAZA

Edificio M

N

0   200 m
0   200 yards

Plataforma del Sur

500 BC showing naked men and women in gesturing poses that earned them the name of 'dancers'. They have puzzled archaeologists for years. Some appear to be swimming, others are deformed, or are apparently cut open to expose their organs. Some have beards or negroid features alien to the Zapotecs, but similar to some Olmec faces. They may represent prisoners of war. One theory is that they are a kind of medical textbook, illustrating illnesses and surgical operations.

The arrow-shaped structure at this end of the plaza (Building J) is angled eastward and has a star symbol on its base, giving rise to the idea that it was aligned to serve as an observatory. Carvings of upside-down (i.e. defeated) men, and hieroglyphic symbols on the walls, however, support the argument that it was a monument to military conquests. Monte Albán writing is different from the glyphs of the Olmecs and Mayas and has not been completely deciphered.

The view from the top of the partly excavated **South Platform** is superb. You can see three mountain ranges converging on Oaxaca. The eastern line of buildings is called **El Palacio**, for its rooms might have been a palatial residence. In the centre of the plaza are the remains of a temple and its staircase. As you leave the complex, on your right you'll see a small ball court. The stone 'seats' on one side seem too narrow for spectators. Were they part of a game? More Mexican mysteries proving that 'nothing is more difficult to predict than the past'.

There's a museum exhibiting carvings and models that help explain Monte Albán's successive phases and its relations with the contemporary cultures of Teotihuacán and the Mayas. Some 500 years after the city's unexplained abandonment, the Mixtec tribe moved into the valley and ruled over the Zapotecs. They used Monte Albán as a cemetery, sometimes appropriating Zapotec graves. When the Aztecs dominated Mexico, the Mixtecs retreated to the hills, where they live today, while the Zapotecs stayed on in the valley. There are good crafts shops and a cafeteria in the museum. Monte Albán is open from 9 a.m. to 5 p.m. Mini-buses from Oaxaca run direct to Monte Albán from the Hotel Mesón del Angel at Calle Mina 518.

OAXACAN COAST

Oaxaca State's Pacific Coast is destined for major development. For years surfers have known about **Puerto Escondido**. Curling breakers they call 'the Mexican Pipeline' attract adepts from all over the Americas. The little town's curving beach, where fishermen land their boats and sell their catch on the spot, its comfortable and informal hotels, good seafood restaurants, shops and nightlife have a loyal following. You can fly in from Mexico City or

Puerto Escondido, famed for its surf, also boasts pleasant restaurants on its curving beach.

Oaxaca, drive or take a bus along the scenic Mex 175 highway through the mountains from Oaxaca. It's only 250km (155 miles) but takes a full day.

A few hours by boat or down the coast road from Puerto Escondido is laid-back **Puerto Angel**. This place really is a 'sleepy little fishing village'. You'll eat lobster on the beach under a thatched *palapa* shelter and snooze on the sand. Turtles come ashore to lay their eggs in this area. They are an endangered species, so please say 'No' if anyone tries to sell you tortoise shell, turtle oil or turtle stew.

Huatulco, another 40km (25 miles) to the south, is fast becoming one of Mexico's biggest beach resorts. It's got the setting – 35km of coastline on nine bays – and was picked for development by FONATUR, the government agency that created Cancún and Ixtapa. By 1989 the first three major hotels were well established, spearheading plans for 7,600 hotel rooms before the end of the century. A tropical environment for golf, tennis, water sports and fishing, plus all the entertainment and amenities of luxury accommodations and direct flights from US cities, are the big lure.

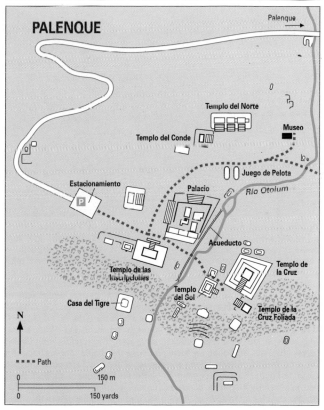

PALENQUE, CHIAPAS

In 1840, the intrepid American explorer, John Lloyd Stephens, and his artist-companion Frederick Catherwood, came down from the Guatemala Highlands into the Mexican state of Chiapas, drawn by rumours of a Maya city in ruins. Near the village of Santo Domingo

Palenque – carved, so it seems, from the jungle that surrounds it – rises tall and mournfully beautiful.

they were led by Indians into the jungle, and soon, to their elation, they were surrounded by massive stones. 'We spurred up a sharp ascent of fragments, so steep the mules could barely climb it ... Through an opening in the trees we saw the front of a large building richly ornamented with stuccoed figures on the pilasters, curious and elegant, with trees growing close against it ... in style and effect it was unique, extraordinary, and mournfully beautiful ... Standing in the doorway, we fired a *feu-de-joie* of four rounds each, using up the last charge of our firearms.'

The ruins of **Palenque** ('tree-surrounded' in Spanish) are still mournfully beautiful, especially when emerging from eddies of mist in early morning. Though major buildings have now been cleared, the grassy setting closely hemmed in by low hills and dense rainforest holds only a fraction of the 500-odd structures so far identified. Walk a few steps along forest paths and you are back in the jungle that still engulfs most of the city. Stephens did not discover Palenque – it had been noted by earlier visitors. But he recognized its difference from the overpowering monumental sites, such as Chichén Itzá. The workmanship is far more artistic and harmonious, less designed to inspire awe.

Palenque's prime spanned 500 to AD 900, the height of the Maya

Classic Period. Nah-Chan (the Maya name, meaning 'house of the serpent') was a city-state ruled by priest-kings, the greatest of whom were **Pacal** and his sons, **Chan-Bahlum** and **Xan-Kul**, who ruled from roughly 615–720 AD. The last dated inscription in Palenque is 799, and sometime after that the city was invaded from the north. It appears to have been largely abandoned in the 9th century.

Nah-Chan was clearly lived in. There are niches with platforms for sleeping and a steam bath. The pagoda-style tower has no counterpart in Mayan architecture. With its large windows commanding a sweeping view of the plain and forest, it may have been a watchtower. At the top of the broad steps to the left of the tower, note the oval relief

The sheer scale of Palenque is awe-inspiring, yet its buildings (here, El Palacio) display harmonious proportions and artistry of the highest kind.

of Pacal seated on a two-headed jaguar throne, receiving the crown from his mother. To the left is the most important of four sunken courtyards, with a hieroglyphic-covered staircase wall. Progress in deciphering Mayan glyphs is being made steadily. In many sites they concentrate on dates and astronomical reckoning – here they detail the ancestry of the ruling family. Around the court's walls are inclined slabs with large-headed figures in relief, perhaps given to Palenque as tribute by vassal towns. The curious bottle-shaped or key-hole recesses were a device to cut down the weight of stone held up by false arches. On the north side, under a shelter, are bits of stucco painted red and green. All of Palenque was originally painted bright red and green.

Just south of the Palacio is the **Templo de las Inscripciones**, an eight-tiered pyramid. Its 69 steps lead to a temple whose 'inscriptions' are hieroglyphics, giving Pacal's pedigree. Chan-Bahlum is also represented on the pillars. This pyramid, handsome enough in itself, turned out to be unique – in 1952, the government archaeologist, Alberto

Ruz l'Huillier, lifted one of the unusual paving stones of the temple and discovered a rubble-filled staircase. After four seasons of digging out stone and mortar to a depth of 21m (70ft), Ruz came to a chamber where a stone box held some jade ornaments and a pearl. Battering through a wall 4m (12ft) thick, the workers found another room and in it a casket containing the skeletons of six young men, evidently sacrificed to guard a tomb. But where was the tomb? A huge triangular stone blocked one wall. Digging around it, Ruz broke into a third chamber and what he saw was 'a huge magic grotto carved out of ice, the walls sparkling and glistening like snow crystals. Delicate festoons of stalactites hung like tassels of a curtain,

Friezes in the courtyard of El Palacio.

and the stalagmites on the floor looked like the drippings of a great candle ... Across the walls marched stucco figures in low relief.' In the centre of the vaulted room, now opened for the first time in more than a thousand years, was a large slab carved with a jewel-draped figure wearing a feathered crown – the excited archaeologists brought jacks to lift the 5-tonne slab. Another stone lid underneath was then removed. In a narrow sarcophagus lay the skeleton of Lord Pacal, his face covered with a mask of jade mosaic. The body was surrounded by jade ornaments, and wore a collar, rings and ear ornaments of jade. In a scene reminiscent of the opening of Tutankhamen's tomb in Egypt, Ruz had discovered the only known

Mayan pyramid built for a royal burial. The 'ice' and 'snow' were crystals from centuries of lime deposits.

The descent into this crypt down slippery steps is not all that pleasant on a crowded tour. At the bottom the carved slab lies in the centre of a room 10m (30ft) long. A strange mortared duct leads from the tomb to the top of the stairs. It is believed to have been a way for Pacal's spirit to speak to the living world. The large,

A unique building in Mayan history, the Templo de las Inscripciones revealed its secret in 1952, when the sarcophagus of Lord Pacal was unearthed by the archeologist Alberto Ruiz l'Huillier.

113

heavy slab had to have been placed there before the pyramid itself was finished, so the entire structure was likely built while Lord Pacal was still alive and made ready for his burial. The ornaments found in the tomb had been placed in the Museum of Anthropology in Mexico City but were stolen in 1985. The treasure was recovered and the museum's exhibit in a reconstruction of the tomb has now been reopened. A stone in the grass before the pyramid marks the grave of Alberto Ruz, facing the tomb he discovered.

A small stream which the Maya had paved over separates El Palacio from an amphitheatre formed at the jungle's edge by the mounds of the **Group of the Cross**, four beautiful 7th-century temples erected by Chan-Bahlum. The largest, on the left, is the **Temple of the Cross** (Templo de la Cruz), so called because of the cross-shaped tree of life design. To the right is a relief panel of a God of the Dead in a jaguar cloak, smoking a cigar; to the right Chan-Bahlum in leggings and a *quetzal* feather headdress. The crests of these temples are called 'roof combs'. The mansard slope of the roofs peculiar to Palenque copies thatch roofs still used today. The **Temple of the Foliated Cross**

The rolling hillsides of Los Altos de Chiapas, near San Cristóbal de las Casas.

(Templo de la Cruz Foliada) straight ahead has key-hole arches and a panel with a leafy tree of life. The roof comb of the facing **Temple of the Sun** (Templo del Sol) is well preserved and so are the heavy stucco external friezes. Inside, a ramrod Chan-Bahlum faces an underworld god against a heraldic device of shields and lances. The word in Maya for shield is *pacal*, the dynasty's name. The small temple is

called **Temple XIV** – here we find the ruler dancing before a kneeling female figure, presenting an offering.

Beyond the Palacio, the outlines of the ball court are visible and farther on are five temples called the **Northern Group**, whose purpose is not known. To the left of this group is the **Templo del Conde**. A picaresque character named Baron Waldeck lived in its ruins in 1832. He was employed by the Irish Lord Kingsborough to help prove the theory that the Mayas were the Lost Tribes of Israel. Kingsborough, like many others, refused to believe that such a civilization could have been created without influence from the western world. He rode his hobby horse into bankruptcy and died in debtors' prison.

A small museum in the trees past the Northern Group must be visited, if only to see the superb terracotta

Ejidos

President Lázaro Cárdenas won great popularity by transferring some 20 million hectares (50 million acres) to poor peasants in the late 1930s. A third of the population received land, and most of it went to ejidos, traditional collectives in which all property was shared by the community.

Ejidos did not get the best land, however, and over the years populatioİn growth meant that ejido families had smaller and smaller parcels to cultivate. Economical large-scale agriculture was not possible on the more than half of arable land held in ejidos and they have become increasingly under-productive and under-financed. The country now imports 10 million tonnes of grain, mostly maize, from its neighbour, the US.

For years ejido land has been untouchable. It could not be sold or transferred. The system was so closely identified with the goals of the Revolution – land for the people – that until President Salinas came along, no one dared to challenge it. In 1991, the President began to initiate reforms needed to rehabilitate this aspect of Mexican agriculture. It will take time and possibly constitutional changes.

To help the rural poor, Salinas has also set up a $2 billion 'Solidarity' fund to finance neighbourhood projects throughout the country.

portrait head of a Maya noble-priest. There is a fine panel of the coronation of Xan-Kul, who followed Chan-Bahlum. One of the figures holding his throne is moustachioed, and since Maya, like most Indians, do not grow facial hair, the presence of bearded faces is always intriguing. Photographs show how the tomb of Lord Pacal looked when it was found. (The museum is open from 9 a.m. to 1 p.m. and from 2 to 5 p.m. The site opens at 8 a.m. and closes at 5 p.m.) *Colectivos* run to and from the ruins and town. Lacandon Indians sell bows and arrows under the trees by a refreshment stand.

The town of Palenque has little of interest to the tourist, but there are hotels, one with a pool. It is possible to rent horses to ride in the surrounding hills and to have a guide lead you on trails where unexcavated ruins loom in the forest. There is a small airport at Palenque but the main airport serving the area is at Villahermosa on the Gulf coast, some two hours away by road. Small planes from both airports can be chartered to visit the important Mayan cities of **Bonampak**, with its famous frescoes, and **Yaxchilán**, both also reachable by fairly arduous road safaris arranged through the hotels. Photographs taken over the years show how the stone and stucco friezes and stelae of Palenque and these jungle cities are steadily being eroded by the acid rain of air pollution.

The bus from Palenque to San Cristóbal de las Casas takes nearly six hours to cover 207km (128 miles) through the gorgeous foothills and **Sierra Madre de Chiapas** mountains of the southernmost Mexican state, Chiapas. This is real jungle, hacked away over much of the road's length by peasants growing maize on the steep hillsides by the ancient slash-and-burn method of land-clearing. One result is heavy soil erosion and landslides that wash out sections of the road every rainy summer. Along the road, women sell bags of oranges and *tacos*. Some 58km (36 miles) out of Palenque the turnoff to **Agua Azul** (Blue Water) leads after 4.8km (2.5 miles) to a nature reserve protecting a staircase of pools with water as blue as the sky. The river spills over projecting limestone platforms, each producing a low, foaming waterfall and a blue basin. The ledges and pools step down the hillside through green forest, an enchanting refuge.

After Ocosingo, as the road climbs, you'll pass ragged coffee plantations where women and children rake beans to dry on the ground. The ferns, elephant-ear plants and tall hardwood trees of the jungle give way to pine forests where wild lantana and dahlias brighten the hillsides. In these parts, nearly every male over the age of 12 seems to carry a machete and wear a straw hat. Mud and thatch huts look very much like the temples atop pyramids in Palenque.

SAN CRISTÓBAL DE LAS CASAS

The charm of **San Cristóbal de las Casas** is its untouristic, strongly Indian flavour. Two Maya tribes predominate in the surrounding villages, the Tzotzils and the Tzeltals, with a few shy Lacandons turning up from the forest on market days. Each village has some identifying trademark in its costumes, but all the men wear knee-length white shorts. The Tzotzil-speaking men of Zinancantán wear hot pink *rebozos* and flat hats trailing ribbons. Their womenfolk wear blue wrap-around skirts and distinctive white *huipiles* embroidered with an ancient intricate Maya rectangular pattern in red. The men wear sandals, but most women go barefoot, and many carry babies in hammock-like *rebozos* slung over their backs. Their hands are always busy, weaving a coloured belt, or making a doll. When seated in the sun, they fold their *rebozos* like bath towels and place them on their head.

The town is old Spanish, though without the flamboyance of the colonial cities of central Mexico, and its history is sombre. The region was invaded in 1527 by a particularly cruel conquistador, Diego de Mazariegos, whom Cortés had sent on a punitive expedition because the local tribes were behind in their tribute payments. Mazariegos founded the town and called it La Villa Real de Chiapas. He captured Indians, branded them and sold them as

117

slaves. This brought him into conflict with Bartolomé de las Casas, a Dominican friar who had sailed with Columbus and had become a staunch protector of the Indians. Las Casas, whose name the town now bears, became bishop of Chiapas in 1545. (You saw him in Diego Rivera's mural in the Palacio Nacional in Mexico City, shaking his cross at the conquistador.) The region had no wealth to attract settlers, and such administration as there was came from Guatemala. Chiapas did not become fully a part of Mexico until after independence in the 19th century.

The houses of San Cristóbal de las Casas have red tile roofs and walls of faded pastel colours, and iron grilles cover the windows. The sidewalks are high; there are big gutters and rainpipes jutting out over the street for the heavy rains. A big doorway usually opens on to an inner patio where family life goes on. Hotels use this arrangement to create flowery courtyards. One of the hostelries was the home of Mazariegos. It can get cold at this altitude (2,262m or 7,465ft) and many hotel rooms have fireplaces.

The Avenida General Utrilla will lead gently upward to the **Santo Domingo** church, a 16th- and 17th-century baroque beauty of buff stone with leafy encrustations on its twisting columns. A quiet gathering of Indian women and their children sit under trees beside the church, weaving and selling their wares. The **Regional Museum** adjoining the church houses a rich exhibit of the textiles and embroidery patterns of Chiapas villages. Present-day examples of these same crafts are sold across the street at a cooperative representing the women of 20 villages, **Sna Jolobil** (Tzotzil for 'house of weaving'). Along this street are shops selling men's leather belts, machetes, baskets made from armadillo armour, bags, *sarapes* and wool rugs.

At the top of the rise, the **Mercado** spreads out for many blocks in the open air around a market building. It is a refreshingly authentic scene, vivid with the costumes of the surrounding villages, the scents and colours of their produce, the squeals and squawks of their animals and the sing-song sibilance of Tzotzil. Tourists are warned quite seriously not to photograph these Indians without their permission. Good photographs of the Indians are sold in book and postcard form at the **Casa Na Bolom Centre** at the upper end of Calle Vicente Guerrero. They are taken by Gertrude Blom, a Swiss photographer-anthropologist-ecologist and widow of the Maya expert Frans Blom, who has made her house a base for scholars and archaeologists for many years. You may visit the library, collections and shop. Don't leave town before a climb up **Cerro de San Cristóbal** (St Christopher's Hill) to visit the church there and admire the fine view over the city.

INDIAN VILLAGES OF CHIAPAS

The church and zócalo of San Juan Chamula, in Chiapas.

The nearby Indian villages certainly merit a detour and can be reached either by cab or *colectivo*. To get to **San Juan Chamula**, 8km (5 miles) away, ride from the market in a *colectivo*, along with the unsold chickens. The church, white with bright blue and yellow ornamentation, can only be visited after buying a ticket at the *Municipio* under the arcade to the right of the walled plaza.

Inside, hundreds and hundreds of candles set on a floor carpeted with pine needles provide both light and heat. You may see men facing the altar with a bottle on the floor in front of them. From time to time they will take a swallow from their bottle –

it is hard liquor, and the act is ritual drinking. This ceremony, rooted in the Mayan past, is to 'bring back the spirit' to a person who has lost his appetite for food or for life. The outward signs here are Christian, but Mayan traditions lie just beneath the surface. It is forbidden to photograph in the church or during the dancing at festivals.

Outside, the men in capes carrying staffs are the elected guardians of the shrine. It is an honour to have this responsibility, or *cargo*, even though it is expensive – the *cargo* officers have to pay for the festivals during the year of their service. As a footnote to history, note that San Juan de Chamula and its environs were given to the doughty chronicler of the *Conquista*, **Bernal Díaz del Castillo**.

Zinacantán, a few miles further on, is a ceremonial centre, also guarded by *cargo* officers. These village squares are packed with dancers on feast days. (Inquire at the Tourist Information Office in San Cristóbal de las Casas for dates and times.) Horseback rides from town can also be arranged. It is pleasant to walk one way, past small farms and orchards, by streams where women are doing the wash and through stretches of woodland, and then ride the *colectivo,* back in the other direction to Zinacantán for a coffee.

The closest airport to San Cristóbal de las Casas is in the Chiapas capital, **Tuxtla Gutiérrez**. The 90-minute trip passes through mountainous terrain where coffee and flowers are grown. Off go the sweaters as you drop down to 530m (1,738ft). Short side trips off this road worth considering are to **Chiapa de Corzo**, 16km (10 miles) outside Tuxtla Gutiérrez. Chiapa de Corzo is a very old village most famous for its lacquered masks and gourds, sold around the zócalo and in the shop of the small **Museo de la Laca**. The dammed Grijalva River, also called the Río Grande de Chiapas, backs up into a lake and the spectacular narrow **Sumidero Gorge**, with walls more than 1,000m (3,000ft) high. You can ride a boat

down the gorge and back from Chiapa de Corzo in a couple of hours, or view the fjord-like scenery from **El Sumidero** lookout on a road from Tuxtla Gutiérrez. (There are in fact two airports in Tuxtla Gutiérrez, one 25 minutes out of town serving Mexico City and the other closer in for Oaxaca flights. Be sure your taxi or bus driver knows which one you're going to.)

VILLAHERMOSA AND LA VENTA

Villahermosa, the capital of the petroleum-producing state of Tabasco, is on the southeastern edge of Olmec territory. The countryside is a watery world of green swamps and trails of brown meanders left in the wake of the Grijalva River, where gas flares glow from high pipes in the oil fields.

La Venta, now hard to reach in the marshes, was an important Olmec centre where a number of the huge helmeted stone heads and innumerable fine works of art dated between 900–400 BC have been found. Excavations at the site were started in 1925 by the archeologist Frans Blom (see p118) and the ruins later came under the protection of Carlos Pellicer Cámera, a poet, historian and archeologist. The environment of the site, mosquitoes and all, has been recreated at the **La Venta Park Museum**, (Parque-Museo La Venta) not far from the Villahermosa Airport and the bus

station for Palenque (a two and a half-hour drive from Villahermosa). The sculptures are tucked away on paths through a very realistic jungle. Deer and other animals wander in the undergrowth where a few crocodiles are installed in pools for atmosphere. The big heads have different faces. Could they have been portraits? The resemblance to negroid features continues to puzzle scientists. The largest head is 2m (7ft) high and weighs 24 tonnes. Look for the altar numbered '6' on the path. A figure reminiscent of the great 'wrestler'

sculpture in the Museo de Antropología of Mexico City, holds a knife and two prisoners by a rope, one with distinctly non-Olmec features. The park is open from 8 a.m. to 4 p.m., closed Monday.

Downtown, the museum of the **Centro de Investigaciones de Culturas Olmecas y Maya**, better known as the CICOM, or Carlos Pellicer Museum, has a remarkable collection of Olmec and Maya treasures. Look for the exquisite terracotta figurines from Maya graves on the island of **Jaina** near Campeche.

121

MAYALAND

Yucatán is Mayaland. The peninsula that Mexico shares with Guatemala and Belize holds the astonishing ruined cities of the final days of a civilization that reached its peak while Europe was sunk in the Dark Ages, then inexplicably and abruptly disappeared. Although most of the great urban centres were abandoned before the arrival of the Spaniards, the people remain. With faces mirroring those on ancient monuments, Mexican Mayans of today thinly populate a territory the size of Great Britain.

Yucatán is different from the rest of Mexico. Where elsewhere all is mountainous, Yucatán is flat as a tortilla, a piece of the ocean floor pushed upward between the Gulf of Mexico and the Caribbean Sea millions of years ago. This limestone slab is porous, quickly absorbing rainfall. Top soil is thin and poor and

Fresh flowers for sale.

there are no rivers. This is one reason the Caribbean waters are so exceptionally clear: no silt muddies them, whilst the limestone and coral reefs make for long beaches of fine white sand.

Underground caverns, like bubbles in the slab, drip their lime in fantastic formations. When the roofs of these caves collapse and expose pools of groundwater, the sinks are open wells called cenotes. These became natural focal points for Mayan communities more than two thousand years ago. There were hundreds of cities and towns then, many of considerable size. **Uxmal** and **Chichén Itzá** have been the most extensively excavated. Chichén Itzà, full of Toltec elements introduced after an invasion from the north around AD 900, represents the last burst of Mayan glory before its eclipse.

Yucatán has always been outside the mainstream, resisting central rule, whether by the Aztecs, the Spaniards or the post-Independence governments in Mexico City. Because it had no gold or silver and its soil was poor, it did not attract many of the conquistadors. In the colonial period it was run as the private domain of Spanish settlers and ranchers. Plantations of agave, the source of henequen fibre for rope, made them rich. An uprising by the Mayan peasants who worked these fields, the **Caste War**, briefly reconquered most of the Peninsula for the Indians between 1847–1849.

Desperate landowners tried to get the United States to intervene and take over Yucatán – instead, Mexican soldiers did the job. Fully a part of Mexico thereafter, it was nevertheless cut off, with scant overland links to the rest of the country.

Interest in Mayan ruins was aroused in the mid-19th century by the books of an American travel writer, John L. Stephens, illustrated by an English artist, Frederick Catherwood, whose detailed drawings of the sites helped guide archaeologists who began serious work in the 1920s. Nevertheless, Yucatán's eastern section, Quintana Roo, did not become a state until 1974. That was the year **Cancún** opened and the Caribbean coast of Yucatán was launched as one of the most popular tourist destinations in the world. It pulls in a million visitors a year.

CAMPECHE

Campeche, capital of the eponymous state on the western flank of Yucatán, was visited by Hernández de Córdoba on a 1517 expedition that marked the route for Cortés two years later. It was Yucatán's main port from 1540 onward. Pirates repeatedly sacked the city until it was enclosed by a thick wall with eight forts in the 17th and 18th cen-

turies. A lot of the wall and seven forts (*baluartes*) remain along the Avenida Circuito de Baluartes to define the colonial character of Campeche's seafront. Several of them house museums. Walking the narrow streets of the centre brings the feel of a citadel city to life. It's a steamy, langourous town. Shrimp boats unload on the docks and freighters take aboard timber. Offshore oil, however, is becoming the biggest business. Look for Panama hats from Becal in the market and shops. The ruins of **Edzna** are the most important of numerous accessible Mayan cities in the vicinity of Campeche. Mérida is 195km

(120 miles) away by the short route, Highway 180, but can also be reached taking in Uxmal and Kabah via Highway 261.

MÉRIDA

Mérida, the gateway to Yucatán, is a charming city of blazing white colonial buildings and quaint 19th-century mansions. These were the homes of millionaire henequen planters. Each seems an attempt to outshine its neighbour, with wrought iron gates, broad palm-studded lawns and turrets with gingerbread trim. When plastics replaced natural fibre after World War II, the henequen wealth dried up. Some of the great houses are now occupied by offices and the excellent regional museum. You can take them in on a tour of the city by open bus or horse-drawn carriage along the tree-lined Paseo Montejo and the city streets linking small plazas and parks.

The Montejos, father and son, settled Yucatán, founding Mérida in 1541 after many battles with the stubborn Mayans, who were not under the illusion that the invaders were gods. The entrance to the **Montejo Palace**, now a bank on the south side of the zócalo, is surmounted by a coat of arms and the effigies of two bearded conquistadors standing on the heads of howling Indians.

Uxmal, in Yucatán, is the finest example of a Mayan style called Puuc.

Well might they howl – the zócalo was the centre of their city, named T'ho, now vanished, its stones recycled into the **Cathedral** (also known as Convento de las Monjas) and other colonial structures. The church, begun in 1561, is strikingly chaste – its bare, white-pillared interior was completely stripped during the 19th century Reform period. Across the street, the white two-storey patio of the **Palacio del Gobierno** has blue sky for a roof and interesting murals of Mayan history. The plaza is rather formal, with topiary bushes and a ring of spreading laurel trees. Its benches are S-shaped love seats that look like grinning dentures.

Even-numbered streets run north–south and odd numbers east–west in Mérida. Following Calle 60 north from the zócalo takes you past Cepeda Park, the Third Order Jesuit Church (Iglesia de Jesús), Santa Lucía church and square and Santa Ana church and square, each worth a peek and perhaps a stop for a cool fresh fruit *licuado* drink in a café. It's hot in Mérida, so siestas after lunch and walks in the cool of the evening are in order. Every night the city offers a concert in a different park. There's street dancing in front of the **Palacio Municipal** on the western side of the square on Sunday evenings, and a programme of Yucatecan costumes and folk dancing in the **Plaza Santa Lucía** on Thursday at 9 p.m. The Ballet Folklórico of the University of Yucatán stages a 'Yucatán and its Roots' show of music and dance in the elegantly restored **Teatro Peón Contreras** on Tuesdays at 9 p.m.

Every male in Yucatán seems to wear a *guayabera*, the loose-pleated, embroidered shirt of the tropics, and many women wear the traditional white cotton *huipil* tunic, embroidered at neck and hem. *Huaraches*, shoes of woven leather strips with tire-rubber soles, are part of the costume. You'll find these and many other hard-to-resist crafts at the

Hammocks
In the streets and plazas of Yucatán, hammock-sellers walk around with their merchandise balanced on their heads and piled in their arms. The brightly coloured nets aren't just for tourists – the hamaca *is still the bed in Mayan village houses.*

The cheaper hammocks are made of synthetic fibres and dyes, while the best are woven from fine cotton thread – you can easily tell the difference. The hammock should be tightly woven. Pull it apart to see that the mesh is not widely spaced and to confirm that there are dozens of pairs of strings at each end, brought together in very tight, secure loops for hanging. The total length should be about twice your height. Double hammocks are called matrimoniales. *They should stretch out to a good 3 metres (10ft) or more in width.*

Mercado Municipal at Calles 56 and 67 and surrounding blocks. Look for the Panama hats (*jipis*), and check out the hammocks, both Yucatecan specialties.

Once the most characteristic sound at food stalls was the slap-slap of tortillas being formed by hand. Now customers line up for this staff of life turned out by machines. A measured pat of corn meal is rolled out, carried on a moving belt to a hot griddle, flipped on both sides and delivered in a stack.

Don't miss the **Museo de Antropología** in the former governor's mansion on Pasco Montejo at Calle 43. Look for the explanation of Mayan numbers, a bar-and-dot system, and the exhibit showing how the heads of infants were deformed by binding them between two boards to produce sloping foreheads. To meet Mayan beauty standards, teeth were filed and eyes made crosseyed by dangling a bead before children's eyes (One wonders how this affected the aim of archers!) The museum is open every day except Monday. It's a good preparation for visiting the Mayan sites reached on day trips from Mérida. Other good preparations are a hat and

Traditional crafts in Mexico take a pride of place in many villages.

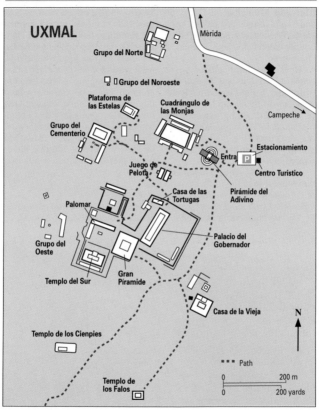

UXMAL

Grupo del Norte

Mèrida

Grupo del Noroeste

Plataforma de las Estelas

Cuadrángulo de las Monjas

Campeche

Grupo del Cementerio

Entra

Estacionamiento

P

Centro Turistico

Juego de Pelota

Pirámide del Adivino

Palomar

Casa de las Tortugas

Grupo del Oeste

Palacio del Gobernador

Templo del Sur

Gran Piramide

Casa de la Vieja

N

Templo de los Cienpies

Templo de los Falos

••• Path

| 0 | 200 m |
| 0 | 200 yards |

sun cream and comfortable rubber-soled shoes for clambering around ruins. Binoculars, a small flashlight and insect repellent may come in handy.

128

UXMAL

The road to **Uxmal**, (pronounced *Oosh-mal*) 82km (50 miles) to the south, goes straight through

Yucatán's low scrub thickets and past some fields of agave. At **Yaxcopoil** you can visit a 17th-century hacienda museum to see how the planters lived and the way henequen fibre is extracted from the agave. The curious little sacks hanging in trees along the way are black oriole nests.

The Uxmal ruins are the finest examples of a Mayan style called **Puuc** (pronounced `pook`), named after the low Puuc hills of this district. It is characterized by rectangular buildings, square columns and an upper frieze panel decorated with intricate projecting geometrical mosaics. Many panels are covered with masks of the rain god **Chaac**, an ugly fellow with a trunk snout and whirly eyes. You'll notice these upper sections are slightly angled outward. The Maya never mastered the true arch, but came close with the **corbel arch** of overlapping stones. Lintels over some doorways are the original sapodilla wood, one carbon-dated at AD 569. The wood is so heavy it doesn't float in water.

Straight ahead as you enter the ruins is the **Pyramid of the Magician** (Pirámide del Adivino). The path from the entrance passes a *chultun*, or cistern to collect rain, the only source of water in this area, which has no cenotes. The rain god was consequently the all-important deity. You approach the steep three-tiered pyramid with rounded corners from the rear and climb 120 steps to the top. There is a safety chain you can hang on to for the climb. (Just don't look back!) The pyramid was built in stages between AD 600–900, each stage covering the preceding one. Moving around to the front side, you'll get a good look at many Chaac masks on the corners of the temple doorway. The door itself is the mouth of a giant mask. From this vantage point you'll see the other principal ruins spread out beneath you and many other still unexcavated mounds in the thick brush beyond.

Directly in front is the **Nunnery** (Cuadrángulo de las Monjas) – names given to Mayan ruins are pure conjecture; no one really knows their purpose – a grassy quadrangle enclosed by four stately low buildings on different levels. On the east, the upper panel of latticework mosaic is decorated with inverted pyramids formed by double-headed serpent bars. The west-side frieze has a stylized snake weaving through it from right to left, with his head between the 6th and 7th doorway.

The more you examine Mayan buildings, the more the tangle of design takes on recognizable shapes. There's a feather canopy crowning a throne above the central door, where the face of an old man with a turtle body can be seen. The north building has a broad staircase used for seating during the evening **Light and Sound Show**. Niches in the façade represent palm-thatched houses. This theme is repeated over the doorways on the south building, where 16 rooms may have been a kind of inn for priests on pilgrimages to Uxmal.

Head south through a corbel arch, and follow a path through the **Ball Court** (Juego de Pelota) to the **Dovecote** (Palomar), so called because of the pierced triangular elements of its roof-comb. It is just one wall of a large, unreconstructed complex to the south. Beside the Dovecote, rubble on three unrestored sides of the **Great Pyramid** (Gran Pirámide) suggests that the Maya were covering it to build a larger one when Uxmal was abandoned around AD 1000. The temple on the top is decorated with very stylized macaws. A small building, rather Grecian in its elegance and harmonious proportions, stands between the pyramid and the ball court. The stone tortoises decorating its upper frieze has earned it the name **House of the Turtles** (Casa de las Tortugas) and it carries the symbolism of fertility and rain.

Continue on to the field fronting the imposing **Governor's Palace** (Palacio del Gobernador). The entire area is a man-made platform. From a distance you'll be able to see that among the thousands of stones making up the façade (all cut without metal tools and fitted without mortar), projecting Chaac heads form an undulating serpent. The fallen column in the plaza is thought to have been used in astronomical observations. There are other partially restored ruins beyond this platform. The **House of the Old Woman** (Casa de la Vieja) is supposed to be the temple of a sorceress who, with her dwarf grandson, the Magician, tricked the king of Uxmal and became rulers of the city. Nearby is a building with phallic rainpipes. Beyond the Dovecote a path leads to the **Cemetery** complex (Grupo del Cementerio), where platforms have skull and crossbone reliefs.

Uxmal's grounds are open from 8 a.m. to 5 p.m. A 45-minute Light and Sound Show in Spanish starts at 7 p.m. followed at 9 by one in English. The dramatized history tells that Uxmal declined because of successive failures of Chaac to deliver the rains and as the result of a war that shifted power to other cities.

There is a good restaurant at the entrance where you can try two Yucatecan specialities, *sopa de lima* ('lime soup', really a hearty chicken and rice soup with tortilla crusts that makes a meal in itself) and *cochinillo pibil* (shredded pork stew with a delicious bitter orange sauce). There are also three hotels near the site, two with swimming pools for cooling off. Within an hour's drive of Uxmal are three other extremely interesting Mayan cities, Kabah, Sayil and Labná. Paved Mayan roads connected these cities.

CHICHÉN ITZÁ

Chichén Itzá, 120km (75 miles) southeast of Mérida, is the best preserved and biggest of the Mayan cities. It may have been settled

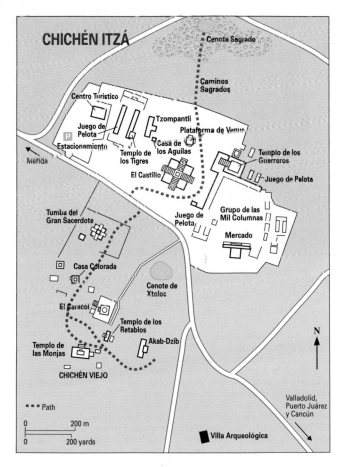

CHICHÉN ITZÁ

Cenote Sagrado

Caminos Sagrados

Centro Turístico

Tzompantli

Plataforma de Venus

Juego de Pelota

P

Estacionamiento

Templo de los Tigres

Casa de los Aguilas

Templo de los Guerreros

Mérida

El Castillo

Juego de Pelota

Tumba del Gran Sacerdote

Juego de Pelota

Grupo de las Mil Columnas

Casa Colorada

Mercado

Cenote de Xtoloc

El Caracol

Templo de los Retablos

N

Templo de las Monjas

Akab-Dzib

CHICHÉN VIEJO

Valladolid, Puerto Juárez y Cancún

▪▪▪ Path

0   200 m

0   200 yards

■ Villa Arqueológica

A sculpture of the Chac-Mool in Chichén Itzá.

around AD 500 by Maya called 'Itzá' moving north from Guatemala. It appears to have been abandoned for the first time 125 years later and re-occupied in about AD 900, after which its most important buildings were constructed. It was to be the last great achievement of Mayan builders. Chichén Itzá was abandoned for good after a war in 1182, though pilgrims continued to visit the Sacred Cenote for centuries. Chichén Itzá in Mayan means 'mouth of the well of the Itzá'.

It is probable that Toltec warriors, perhaps led by the legendary Ce Acatl Topiltzín of Tula, namely, Quetzalcóatl, captured Chichén Itzá around the year 1000. Toltec influences in religion and architecture include the worship of the feathered serpent/morning star god the Mayans adopted as Kukulcán. After the arrival of the Toltecs, the region was increasingly disrupted by inter-city wars, perhaps spurred by the need for prisoners used in the human sacrifices also introduced by the Toltecs. The ruins are in two sections, Old Chichén (Chichén Viejo) and New Chichén, roughly before and after the Toltec conquest.

The Spaniards named New Chichén Itzá's pyramid **El Castillo**. It is in fact a temple to Kukulcán and evidently had importance in Mayan astronomy. There are four flights of stairs with 91 steps on each. Adding the top platform gives 365, the days of the year. The stairs divide nine terraces into 18 on each side, the number of months in the Mayan calendar. At 5 p.m. on the spring and autumn equinoxes, a shadow moves down the right wall of the north staircase like the rippling body of a snake until it reaches the carved serpent head at the base; then it moves back up again – Kukulcán descending to earth and returning to the heavens! The phenomenon understandably attracts large crowds.

There's a narrow stair inside the pyramid built in the 1930s by archeologists. A hot, clammy and crowded climb takes you to the platform of an earlier temple that holds a red-painted jaguar with jade eyes and mother-of-pearl spots. This is no place for the claustrophobic. The north chamber of the temple atop the Castillo is decorated with carvings on columns and reliefs of priests in feathered headdresses.

Directly in front of the north staircase, the **Plataforma de Venus** is full of Toltec influence. The faces carved on the sides, with staring eyes and round ear plugs are not Mayan. You'll find a carving of the Toltec morning star and its symbol, a graceful feathered serpent, around the top level, as well as a curious fish with legs. A tadpole? Traces of red and green paint are a reminder that this city, too, was once resplendently coloured.

To the east stands the **Temple of the Warriors** (Templo de los Guerreros). The portico of square columns richly carved with warriors in armour fronts steep stairs to the top platform where a Chac-Mool is centrally placed. These stylized figures are always the same – a reclining man holding a plate on his lap. They may have been stands for burning incense. The temple doorway is formed by snakes whose rattles bend overhead to hold the vanished lintel. More columns reminiscent of Tula form a portico on the south side of the temple called the **Mercado**, or market. No doubt these colonnades, when roofed, provided relief from the Yucatán sun. The south walls are covered with reliefs of eagles, bears and jaguars. An earlier **Temple of the Chac-Mool** underlies this complex.

A rough causeway some 275m through the undergrowth leads from the Castillo to the **Cenote Sagrado**. It's a haunting spot, a well 59m (192ft) across, overhung with trees and vines. Here human sacrifices were thrown to propitiate the rain god in times of drought. The legend says the victims were beautiful virgins, but most of the more than 40 skeletons found by dredging were of children. A quantity of offerings in jade and gold has been recovered from the steep-sided well's murky green waters, some 22m (65ft) deep. The first attempt was made in 1903 by Edward Thompson, the US vice-consul in Mérida, who bought the whole ruins and hacienda of Chichén Itzá for $75. Some of his loot has been returned to the museum in Mérida; the rest is in US museums. The refreshment stand at this grisly spot seems a bit out of place, as does the annoying roar of planes and helicopters continually ferrying visitors from Cancún to a nearby field.

Returning to the main area, on the right is the **Tzompantli**, a wall of skull reliefs in black and white, also decorated with eagles holding human hearts in their talons, all very Toltec in spirit. Next comes the **Temple of the Jaguars** (Templo de los Tigres), built into the rear wall of the ball court. The reliefs on the lower level columns describe the creation of the world. Tears from the eyes of the god on the left pillar become waters that give life to plants and animals and then to man. The right pillar is a woman with a skull head representing death. This duality of life and death is a constant theme of religious art in Mesoamerica. In the centre of the rear wall covered with warriors is a bearded figure who may be Kukulcán. The doorway of the upper temple is flanked by huge monolithic serpents. Inside are more warriors and fresco fragments of Toltecs fighting with Maya.

The **Ball Court** (Juego de Pelota) is the biggest in Mexico. The price of defeat, or victory (see p22) is vividly described in relief panels at midcourt. A headless captain with serpents streaming like blood from his neck kneels before his opponent, who holds the head and brandishes a knife. Note the protective pads, shoes and costumes of the players.

Old Chichén Itzá is reached by a trail south of the Castillo. All along the way are the mounds of mostly unexcavated structures until you reach one of the city's most unusual buildings, **El Caracol** (the Snail), also called the Observatory. Situated in an open space, this round tower has an interior circular stair leading to the rooms where observations were made of Venus and other heavenly bodies. Farther on, the top-heavy one-room **Iglesia** (Church) and **Templo de las Monjas** (Nunnery) are temples heavily adorned in the Puuc style, with the curling Chaac snouts in evidence. The Nunnery was partly blown up by treasure hunters. The **Casa Colorada** (Red House), on a mound and with remains of a classic Mayan roof comb, is one of the oldest at this site, dated 7th century.

The southern section of the ruins is a 15-minute walk along a small path. Most of the buildings are semi-overgrown. On one, the two **atlantes** holding up a door lintel are obvious copies of the warrior pillars at Tula. Other temples and houses are purely Mayan. Ruins in the brush are found in all directions, giving an idea of the vast extent of Chichén Itzá in its prime. A model and explanations in the Visitor's Centre museum at the entrance are helpful in putting it all in perspective. All this is a lot to appreciate in one day, especially if it is hot. If you want to see the ruins thoroughly, plan to stay at one of the several comfortable hotels adjoining the site.

The **Balankanche** cave 5km (3 miles) from the Visitor's Centre was discovered in 1959 and found to have been used for Mayan rites. It takes a bit of squeezing and stooping to get through to the chambers where offerings to the rain god were made. Jars and an altar have been left as they were found beside a pool where blind fish swim. Tours of the cave leave every hour on the hour from 8 to 11 a.m. and from 2 to 4 p.m., but only morning hours on Sunday. You can swim in the pool of the **Dzitnup Cenote** about 40km (25 miles) east on the highway toward Valladolid. A sunbeam shining through a hole in the ceiling of this cavern lights the sapphire blue of the cool water.

Stop for a stroll in almost any village along the way to Chichén Itzá and notice the oval Mayan houses of mud and wattle, unchanged since ancient times. Yards are swept clean and kitchens are outside. The family sleeps in hammocks. Cemeteries, such as the one at **Holca**, have

brightly coloured little houses as tombs. A detour to **Izamal** will add about an hour's travel time to your trip. The 16th-century Franciscan monastery and huge arcaded courtyard here was the headquarters of Bishop **Diego de Landa**, who collected the books of the Mayas and burned them. He somewhat made up for this atrocity by writing an important record of Mayan history and customs learned from the natives. A small pyramid rises nearby in this pleasant colonial town. Other excursions from Mérida are to the scattered ruins of **Dzibilchaltún** (said to be the oldest settled site in the continent and one of the largest Mayan city in Yucatán) and to the **Río Lagartos National Park**, home of the largest nesting colony of flamingos in Mexico. The ruins are an hour's drive to the north, near the port of Progreso, Mérida's beach. The trip to the park takes a full day, including a boat ride to where thousands of flamingos feed in shallow water.

CANCÚN AND THE COAST

Magnificent Caribbean beaches were the first face of Mexico seen by Europeans, at least as early as 1517. For well over four centuries Quintana Roo, the Caribbean coast of Yucatán, was left to the few rebellious Maya who could scratch a living in the brush; for everyone else it was a remote place of exile. By

135

The peaceful setting of the Río Lagartos National Park provides the perfect habitat for a large colony of flamingoes.

now the story is well known how the government's tourism developers, FONATUR, fed a 'wish list' into a computer to locate the ideal beach. The computer answered 'Cancún'. The uninhabited 22km (14-mile), hook-shaped island had to be developed from scratch, but it had everything nature could provide: an average 243 sunny days a year, a fantastic beach on one side, and a tranquil lagoon on the other. As an added touch, Mayan ruins were not far distant. To construct and service the playground, a new town, Cancún City, was built on the mainland and short causeways connected it to both ends of the island. Only super deluxe hotels were permitted on Cancún (good cheaper ones have risen in the town), and roads and an airport had to be installed. When the luxurious complex opened in 1974, it was no coincidence that Quintana Roo should finally become a state in that same year. Cancún's fame spread

when journalists converged on the island for a political summit in 1982. Today a million vacationers a year visit Cancún, and the airport is Mexico's second busiest.

Cancún belongs to Lotusland, an international country with outposts around the world wherever there is unfailing sunshine and drinks are served in coconut shells. Miami is closer in flying time, and in spirit, than Mexico City. Once you arrive you can forget the real world of yesterday and tomorrow until it's time to pay the bill. The lagoon is for practising your windsurfing, waterskiing

Perpetual sunshine, crystal clear waters, beautiful sandy beaches ... Cancún is a hand-picked holiday resort.

and sailing; pools and the beach are for sunning and swimming. There are many to sample along the length of Cancún's only street, Paseo Kukulcán. Merely lift your hand and a waiter will be there to bring refreshment.

The sporting Lotuslanders take to the tennis courts or the beautiful Robert Trent Jones Pok-ta-Pok golf

The Maya

Of the many tribes that have left their mark on Mesoamerica, the Maya are the most fascinating. The puzzles of their origin and decline have obsessed generations of scholars. Some theorized that they were descended from a 'second ark' launched along with Noah's. Others thought that they were survivors of wrecked ships blown off course from Egypt or Phoenicia or Japan. An Irish nobleman spent his fortune trying to prove that they were a lost tribe of Israel. It is now accepted that they originated in Asia, along with the rest of the Amerindians.

By at least 600 BC the Maya had settled an area that today includes El Salvador, Guatemala, Belize, parts of Honduras, and Yucatán and Chiapas in Mexico. The Classic Period of Mayan civilization came between AD 300 and 900 and centred on imposing sacred cities in the highland jungles, such as Copán in Honduras, Tikal in Guatemala and Palenque in Chiapas. There, a society ruled by priest-kings worked gold and copper, and produced refined objects and hyeroglyphics, a 365-day calendar of great precision and astronomical observations accurate within seconds. Their mathematical system, multiplying by 20s, included the concept of zero and fixed the 'beginning of time' at 12 August 3113 BC.

In the north of Mayaland, the lowland Maya in Yucatán built their urban centres toward the end of the Classic Period, but continued longer, combining with an influx of Toltecs from the central highlands of Mexico. The highland cities were emptied around AD 900, the lowland centres around AD 1200. What happened? The experts disagree. Some say that increasing populations exhausted the poor soil and droughts brought starvation. Others postulate peasant revolts at the labour involved in city-building. Epidemics and invasions are also suggested. In any case, the Maya were still living in cities, such as Tulum, when the Spaniards arrived. They have survived. Today, Mayan is the first language of some 250,000 Indians in Mexico and many more thousands in countries to the south.

*Recently, an international project called **La Ruta Maya** has been forming among five different nations (original homelands of the Maya – El Salvador, Guatemala, Belize, Honduras and Mexico). Designed as a 2, 500km (1,500-mile) route through ancient Mayan country, La Ruta Maya also refers to an inter-regional plan to protect the environment while showcasing the shared historical and archaeological heritage.*

The pressures of a growing population along with the devastation caused by careless tourist development have awakened officials to the need for more planning. La Ruta Maya includes the creation of parks and conservation areas as well as environmentally sensitive tourism and transportation along the way, such as a proposed monorail through tropical rainforest.

course. They go scuba diving and deep-sea fishing on cruisers or take a mini-sub to get close-up photographs of a wrecked ship and brilliantly coloured tropical fish in their silent dream world. There's even a small Mayan ruin, **El Rey**, behind the Camino Real Hotel. The Maya evidently recognized Cancún as special, too. A museum in the white-domed **Convention Centre** exhibits a modest collection of antiquities.

Lotuslanders shop in boutiques with famous names, in the mall at the Convention Centre or among the handicraft stalls of the **Mercado de Artesanías** on Tulum Boulevard in Cancún City, where the products of all Mexico are assembled for them – Cancún is a duty-free zone. For Mexicans, this means considerable reductions from their 10 per cent IVA tax. Foreigners won't see great savings on imported luxuries. For some final authentic colour, there's a bullring in town, with corridas from December to April.

By night, a whiff of Mexico is imported for Mexican fiesta programmes at the hotels and the folkloric dinner show at the Convention Centre. Of course there's no lack of clubs for the disco scene and bar-hopping.

Many Lotuslanders never leave Cancún except to head back to the airport. If you insist on seeing Mexico, or just want to give your sunburn a rest, your hotel can arrange short excursions by land or small plane to the great Mayan city, Chichén Itzá, or by bus or rented car to the ruins of Tulum. Short flights or fast ferries go to nearby Isla Mujeres and Cozumel.

The Tulum trip down the coast passes a string of marvellous beaches, some completely untouched, others with bungalows or palm-thatched *palapa* shelters for hammock-slinging, and a few with first-class hotels catering to scuba divers.

If you're in your own car you can make short detours to these. **Punta Bete**, 60km (37 miles) south of Cancún has good swimming off a picture-postcard beach with coconut palms and turquoise waters. **Akumal**, after 104km (65 miles) is famed for diving. There's an underwater museum where you can swim among cannons and other artifacts found by divers. The first-class club-hotel has a good restaurant. **Xcacel** (pronounced *sha-SELL*) is also a very attractive uncrowded swimming beach.

All buses stop at **Xel-ha Lagoon** (*shell-HA*), a national park. Jungle comes down to the coral ledge that encloses this limpid lake from the sea. The water is only slightly salty, so you can swim with your eyes open to watch the countless varieties of fish. There's a restaurant, picnic grounds, a bazaar, changing rooms and places to rent snorkel gear and underwater cameras. It is a very special place – it's just a shame there are so many buses.

139

Cozumel's coral barrier reef is a heaven for swimmers, snorkellers or divers.

TULUM

When the chronicler of the conquest, Bernal Díaz del Castillo, saw the towers of **Tulum** from the sea in 1518, he compared them to Seville, an exaggeration that somewhat clouds his credibility. By Mayan standards it was a small trading city,

built around 1200 when Mayan architecture had become decadent. Surrounded by a wall with five gates, it most probably had to be defended during the wars that contributed to the decline of the Maya in Yucatán.

Tulum's glory is its setting. The **Castillo**, the central temple on a high platform, commands an incomparable view over the sea and coast. Perfect little beaches spread out below. The deity worshipped in Tulum was **Yumkin**, the 'Descending God', always shown diving head first on these buildings. It is thought he represented the setting sun. Central to Mayan religion was the fear that the setting sun might never return from his journey into the underworld. The **Temple of the Frescoes**, in the centre of the compound, has faded paintings inside and out of offerings to the god; also fish and fertility figures. A stucco relief of Yumkin holding a snake fills a niche by the door. Notice how the cornice angles form faces. Yumkin is seen again over the entrance to his own temple to the left of the Castillo. The **Temple of the Sun and the Moon** looks like a great open fireplace. A stucco sculpture of two joined bodies may have given the temple its name. There are many mounds of buildings not considered worth reconstructing within the site.

Of special interest is a stretch of ancient road dividing the compound. Though they didn't have wheeled vehicles, the Mayans did build paved roads, called *sacbes*, perhaps for ceremonial processions. More of these may be seen at **Coba**, a very interesting 8th-century Mayan site on lakes some 40km (25 miles) inland. A network of *sacbes* crosses Coba's mostly unexcavated ruins, which extend for kilometres into the jungle. (One of the roads paved with crushed rock is 10m (30ft) wide and runs 100km (62 miles) to another Mayan centre.) Coba was evidently a very large city, probably founded by Maya from Guatemala, for the very steep pyramids here – the tallest

in Yucatán – are similar to the ones at Tikal. At Coba you can share the archaeologist's feelings of discovery as you follow jungle trails surrounded by mysterious mounds. Bring insect repellent and wear walking shoes.

ISLA MUJERES AND COZUMEL

Although only 10km (6 miles) from Cancún, **Isla Mujeres** is quite another world. No local Amazons gave the little island its name, but rather fertility idols found by Cortés in 1519. Today it is favoured by young and budget-conscious vacationers who come over on the ferries from Puerto Juárez just north of Cancún or Punta Sam (cars carried), or by small plane from Mérida or Cancún. Swimmers head for **Playa los Cocos**, snorkellers for **El Garrafón**'s coral reef. A curiosity for expert divers only are the underwater caves where 'sleeping' sharks lie on the bottom and, survivors claim, can even be handled. The island is only a 2km wide and 8km (5 miles) long, but is fairly crammed with hotels, shops and seafood restaurants.

Cozumel lies near the northern end of a barrier reef of coral that is second only to Australia's. Quintana Roo has no rivers pouring sediment into the sea, no fertilized farmlands and few communities to pollute the coast. The coral reef produces white sand and prevents waves from roiling the bottom. The result is water of crystalline clarity, a light aquamarine blue, or golden green, according to the sun and sky. Its temperature is warm but not tepid. In other words, absolute heaven for swimmers, snorkellers and divers. Most hotels rent the necessary equipment. If you're reluctant to snorkel, you can take a glass-bottomed boat tour.

Cozumel is roughly 50km long and 15km wide (30 x 9 miles) and its close proximity to Cancún has enabled the island to keep touristic development relatively low-key.

A proficiency card is required for scuba diving, but instructors will deliver one after alarmingly few hours and will act as guides on reefs of varying complexity. **Palancar Reef** is 5km (3 miles) long and drops sharply into a 1,620m, mile-deep trough with 75m (250ft) visibility. **San Francisco Reef**, about 545m (500yd) long and 15m (50ft) deep is easier, and **Yacab**, 9m (30ft) deep is fine for beginners. Boats to the reefs and **Chancanab National Marine Park** stop at hotel docks to pick up passengers and provide refreshments and even gear.

The underwater population is gaudy: delicate blue angel fish, black and white striped sergeant majors, red squirrel fish with big eyes and a spiny back, intense, electric-coloured

The beach at Chetumal, in Quitana Roo.

schools of tiny wrasse dazzling like a cloud of sparks, butterfly fish with a round black spot, yellow and silvery grunts, and rainbow-hued parrot fish are just a few of the common varieties close to shore. Farther out you might see a ray flap by like a giant bird. The natural aquarium at Chancanab is a good place to learn to identify the varieties and to get quite close enought to a moray eel. One hotel boasts an airplane underwater, put there for filming a movie.

With all this in a calm sea, fewer people swim in the hotel pools. Poolside is great for sunning, socializing and snacking. Beachside, there s tennis, windsurfing, parasailing, chasing about on the noisy waverunners and sailing, as well as cycling. Charter boats go out for game fish from the harbour of **San Miguel**. A marlin tournament is held in May.

The hotels are fairly spaced apart on the western side of the 45km (28-mile) long island. You can drive around it in a couple of hours, passing a variety of beaches, from reef-protected to pounding surf. Near mid-point, iguanas scuttle in the modest Mayan ruins at **San Gervasio**. Turtles come ashore in July to lay eggs near **Punta Molas**. Don't buy black coral – it only comes from this area and is now so hard to find that divers must go down 75m (246ft) to get it.

San Miguel is basically a giant shopping mall interspersed with a few lively restaurants and bars, where margaritas are served in goblets the size of mere goldfish bowls. The din of rock music from radios is constant and traffic gets noisy along the seafront Malecón. The Maya did not have the wheel; Mexican cars don't seem to have mufflers. Hotels offer evening entertainment, but while there are discos in town, Cozumel isn't really big on nightlife. Do as the locals do: join the crowd at outdoor tables around the zócalo and walk back to your hotel escorted by fireflies.

In winter, cruise ships unload up to 2,000 passengers a day in an assault on the shops of San Miguel, where most Mexican handicrafts and some designer clothes are found. Shop owners put up permanent signs reading 'Welcome passengers of the ———' and hang up a new ship's name every day. San Miguel is a consumer's paradise. Prices are quoted in dollars, which are practically a second coin of this realm.

Same-day tours to Xel-ha, Tulum and Coba are easily arranged. It is customary to tip the guide. A ferry connects with buses at **Playa del Carmen** on the mainland, which incidentally has a very nice beach and some good budget accommodation. Small-plane flights to Chichén Itzá are also available from Playa del Carmen. The Cozumel airport began as a US Navy anti-submarine base in World War II. Now it receives passengers direct from US and Mexican cities and connects with Europe through Miami.

SILVER CITIES

For colonial atmosphere, the 'Silver Cities' are pure gold. The Spaniards never found the legendary city of El Dorado but they did discover ores in the mountains northwest of Mexico City that poured out a river of silver for centuries and continue to make Mexico *número uno* in world production. Throughout the 17th and 18th centuries, while Indian labour slaved in the mines, immensely rich mine-owners lavished fortunes on handsome cities literally built on silver. They embellished them with splendid churches, public buildings and stately mansions for themselves. But these wealthy families were mostly *criollos*, born in Mexico of Spanish descent, and as such not entitled to hold the political offices reserved for the *peninsulares*, born in Spain. Early in the 19th century *criollos* plotted to throw out the royalist *peninsulares* and for a time they made common cause with the oppressed Indians and *mestizos* of the mining towns. Thus the Silver

Cities are known as the 'cradle of Mexican independence'. Artists and retirees have been drawn by the charm of their picturesque streets and the mild climate. With them have come attractive hostelries, shops and restaurants.

A circuit of the region can be a highlight of a Mexican journey, or an end in itself. Most travel agencies in Mexico City offer Silver City tours that visit the towns most accessible from the capital – Querétaro, San Miguel de Allende, Guanajuato and Morelia – extendable by a variety of interesting side trips. First-class buses and a fast train, the Constitucionalista, serve the area, too.

From the capital, an express toll road, Highway 57D, reaches Querétaro in three hours. (This is also the route to Tepotzotlán and Tula, see pp83–5.) You can leave the autoroute just short of Querétaro to spend a pleasant hour in **San Juan del Río**, a trim, white colonial town where many shops sell opals mined in the region. Another 12km (7.5 miles) leads to quaint **Tequisquiapan**, where hotels and public pools offer baths fed by radioactive hot springs, said to be good for arthritis. It's a popular spa, with good shops, riding and a golf course.

QUERÉTARO

The outskirts of **Querétaro** are industrial, but you should press on to the zócalo's trimmed laurel trees and the surrounding colonial-period streets closed to traffic. Down Calle Madero is the **Santa Clara church**, whose simple outside hides a brilliantly florid interior. The Churrigueresque altar screen is a masterpiece of carving and gilding. The Neptune fountain next to the church is by Eduardo Tresguerras, a 'Renaissance man' as a leading architect, sculptor and painter of 18th-century Mexico. Tresguerras is responsible for the arched aqueduct running into the city centre, still in use. A block west on Calle Allende is Querétaro's pride, the **Palacio Federal**. This former Augustinian convent's elaborate façade and courtyard encrusted with sculptures in the late Baroque style was completed in 1743. It is now a post office.

Down every street in the historic centre you will discover churches with yellow and blue tile cupolas, and mansions with forged iron gates and arched entries into intriguing patios. On Calle 5 de Mayo at Plaza de la Independencia, the **Casa de la Corregidora** (now the City Hall) is one of many landmarks dedicated to the wife of a Querétaro councilman who, in 1810, tipped off conspirators for independence that their plot had been discovered. La Corregidora's warning enabled Father Hidalgo to advance the timing and launch the revolt from his parish church in Dolores.

The **Regional Museum**, in the harmonious premises of a former Franciscan convent on Calle Corregidora across from the zócalo recalls other historic events. After Juárez defeated Maximilian's army outside Querétaro in 1867, the emperor was condemned to death by a court that met in the **Teatro de la República**. The execution by firing squad took place nearby on the **Cerro de las Campanas**, the Hill of Bells. The spot is marked by a rather hideous statue of Juárez and a small Habsburg chapel. The Constitution of 1917 was signed in the Teatro de la República.

SAN MIGUEL DE ALLENDE

San Miguel de Allende has no silver mines but it became rich as a market centre servicing the mining communities. The town of some 50,000 is special because it has kept its original appearance intact. You come upon it from above, and the road looks down on spires of pink stone, domes of coloured majolica, white walls and rosy roof tiles. The whole, perfect ensemble is protected as a national monument where no modern buildings may intrude. Cobbled lanes descend to the **Plaza Allende**, and a most unexpected 1880 Gothic-style church. **La Parroquia** expresses the fantasies of an Indian mason and architect, Zeferino Gutiérrez, who is supposed to have taken his inspiration from a postcard image of a French cathedral.

A tour of the square quickly reveals that San Miguel has attracted a

147

sizeable colony of *Yanqui* residents, at home in the sidewalk cafés, shops and attractive restaurants. Many are students or dabblers at the **Instituto Allende**, an art and language school on the Avenida San Antonio, or the **Bellas Artes Centro Cultural**, in an 18th-century cloister at Calle Hernández Macías 75. The influence of these schools may well be responsible for the profusion of shops selling well-designed jewellery and crafts in silver, tin, brass, mirrors and glass.

San Miguel de Allende boasts numerous interesting colonial monuments, but it's really a place for leisurely wandering, good shopping and candlelit dinners in animated cafés with Mexican music. And the numerous cozy hotels installed in old houses make it a good base for exploring the region. House-and-garden walking tours that give you a rare glimpse of the hidden opulence leave from the *biblioteca* (library) Sunday mornings at 11.30 a.m. Don't miss the **Oratorio** church on a platform above the local market or its adjoining chapel in back, holding the tombs of the Conde de la Canal and his wife.

The Canal family built grand houses in the town, but San Miguel's most famous son is **Ignacio Allende**, one of the heroes of the 1810 uprising for independence. San Miguel's name was extended to honour him. His house, on Calle Cuna de Allende just off the zócalo, is a museum furnished in period style.

GUANAJUATO

Guanajuato is capital of the state of the same name. The 90-minute drive from San Miguel de Allende passes through the rolling plains of the fertile **Bajío** district. You'll see farmers ploughing with oxen, boys trotting by on *burros*, hay stacked in trees (out of the reach of animals) and lots of feathery pepper trees with their inedible red fruit. The peak of **El Cubilete** in the Sierra Madre Occidental stands out on the horizon, surmounted by a tall statue of Christ. It is called the geographical 'centre' of Mexico.

Guanajuato is tucked deep in the folds of a river gorge encircled by rounded hills. The topography defeats the grid pattern of most Mexican towns. Streets and alleys tumble down steep slopes and twist about among small irregular plazas in a bowl bright with colour. The houses stepped down the canyon walls are painted in softly glowing shades and almost all have balconies overflowing with flowers. There's a competition in May for the prettiest. As you descend, the road suddenly plunges into a tunnel, the *subterráneo*, a snaking, arched 1.5km-long freeway partly underground that moves traffic rapidly

La Parroquia, San Miguel de Allende's cathedral, is an incongruous landmark of the city.

instead of clogging the narrow by-ways above. Until the river was paved over and diverted, floods regularly inundated the lower districts, where highwater marks can be seen on the walls.

Driving in town is hopeless; park in a hillside garage above the **Jardín de la Unión**, the hub of the city. Laurel trees grow entwined to shade this small zócalo. Side-by-side across the street are the **Teatro Juárez**, a 1903 extravaganza in the French style dear to the dictator Porfirio Díaz, and the delicately decorated 18th-century pink stone **San Diego** church. Following this street leads up to the Plaza de la Paz, hemmed in by imposing mansions and the **Basílica de Nuestra Señora**

Tucked in the folds of a river gorge, Guanajuato tumbles into narrow streets redolent of the past.

La Compañía, the church of the Jesuits who founded the university. It is Guanajuato's finest example of 18th century super-baroque. Note the beautifully carved doors and the exceptionally fine dome.

On the other side of the university, Calle Pocitos leads to the **Museo del Pueblo de Guanajuato**, lodged in the palace of the Marqués de Rayas. The museum is mainly devoted to religious paintings. A more interesting landmark a bit farther down the street at No. 67 is the house where **Diego Rivera** was born in 1896. His evolution from these bourgeois beginnings into a revolutionary painter is interestingly documented in a small museum upstairs.

Follow the street's ups and downs to the **Alhóndiga de Granaditas**. Guanajuato's royalists took refuge in this fortress-like granary in 1810 when the city was attacked by the peasant army led by Father Hidalgo. An Indian miner called Pípila managed to set the door on fire before being shot. Then the mob rushed in and hacked the people inside to death. When the tide later turned, the heads of Hidalgo, Allende and two other independence leaders were hung on hooks on the four corners of this building and stayed there as a warning for ten years. The

de Guanajuato, one of the city's most impressive colonial monuments. The interior is classic, with huge chandeliers and an altar to the Virgin, whose image was given by King Philip II of Spain. It stands, like the city, on a base of silver. Behind the church, the **University of Guanajuato**'s white Moorish front looks old, but isn't. Next door is

151

GUANAJUATO

Alhóndiga is both a shrine to independence and an excellent small museum. A block below in the cavernous **Mercado Hidalgo** you can try to count the different varieties of peppers for sale. Markets in the Bajío farming country are among the most colourful and richly supplied in all Mexico, and Guanajuato's is the Bajío's best. Look for *tomatillos*, little green fruit with a papery skin used in sauces, brown tamarind pods, *nopales*, cactus paddles, *mamey* fruit, several kinds of avocados, the creased green and spiny *chayote*, the 'vegetable pear' that tastes like a delicate squash, fresh coriander leaves and the *epazote* herb with spiky leaves, both essential ingredients in Mexican cooking. The grey-black ears of corn you'll see are deformed by *huitlacoche*, a fungus prized for making a stuffing that tastes like mushrooms. Bright yellow squash blossoms are chopped and fried as filling for folded, toasted tortillas called *quesadillas*. Brown cones are *piloncillos*, raw sugar. Yellow mounds of dough called the *masa* are for tortillas – the dough is made by soaking dried kernels of corn in a solution of unslaked lye, then mashing it. You can sample fruits, buy herbal remedies, eat

mummy-shaped nut candy, and on the balcony above, browse through handicraft stalls.

In October and November Guanajuato hosts one of Mexico's most important cultural events, the International Cervantes Festival. It all began with traditional university stu-

Mexico's fascination with death is no more evident than at the Museo del Panteón, where mummified cadavers are on display behind glass cases.

152

dent performances of short skits, or *entremeses*, by Cervantes staged in the open air in the **Plazuela San Roque** off the Avenida Juárez. Now the three-week programme attracts the world's best orchestras, ballets, theatre groups, singers and chamber musicians, and includes a film festi-val and art exhibits. Every theatre, hall, church and plaza in town is converted into performing space. Ticket and hotel reservations must be made many months in advance.

Following Avenida Juárez back toward the zócalo, you'll come to the Plazuela de los Angeles. Off

Market day in San André Cuetzalan.

this square, on the Callejón del Patrocinio, is an alley, or rather a passage, so narrow that the flower-filled balconies almost touch. It's called the Callejón del Beso, the **Alley of the Kiss**. Guides – and any kid playing in the street becomes one at the sight of a foreigner – reel off a Romeo-and-Juliet yarn here about a rich merchant's daughter and poor boy from the mines who kissed across facing balconies.

The best views of the whole city can be taken in from a road that climbs the canyon walls and encircles the town, the **Carretera Panorámica**. A heroic pink stone statue of the brave **El Pípila** provides one good vantage point. The worst sight in Guanajuato is at the **Museo del Panteón**, the cemetery museum,

on the outskirts. There's usually a line at the ticket counter waiting to see scores of naturally mummified cadavers proppped up in glass cases. In Mexico, grave space is rented to families for fixed periods and these bodies had been evicted by the municipality for non-payment. They have since earned the town much more than they owed.

A few miles out on the road to Dolores Hidalgo, **La Valenciana** church sits on top of what was the richest silver deposit in the world. The Valenciana mine made its owner fabulously rich and earned him a title, the Count of Valenciana. In gratitude, he built in 1788 a perfect gem of Mexican baroque in pink stone dedicated to San Cayetano. Note the finely carved and painted features and robes of the figures on the gilded main altar, each a little masterpiece within the whirling, exalted whole.

155

Guanajuato's mines have produced more than a billion dollars worth of silver ... and they are still at it. You can visit the mine and in the village find shops selling rock crystals and other minerals. Rock hounds won't want to miss the **Museo de Minería** in the School of Mines on this road just above the city. Before leaving Guanajuato, try to visit **Marfil**, on the southern outskirts. Once a mining centre, abandoned because of floods, it is now a cool green oasis where attractive villas and gardens with cypress trees lend an Italian atmosphere. The **Museo Ex-Hacienda San Gabriel Barrera** here is part hotel and part museum in a restored house of a colonial estate. The wife of former President López Portillo restored the property and filled it with beautiful period furniture.

ZACATECAS AND SAN LUIS POTOSÍ

Zacatecas, 325km (200 miles) north of Guanajuato, and **San Luis Potosí**, about 185km (115 miles) farther east, are the outposts of the silver mining region, both steeped in the colonial tradition. Zacatecas is on the border of the arid north, surrounded by bare brown mountains. Its cathedral is considered by many to be Mexico's most beautiful. San Luis Potosí's environs are harsh as well, but the city is an elegant state capital that was also one of the movable capitals of Benito Juárez's outlawed government during the Maximilian years. The Churrigueresque red stone Templo del Carmen and the National Mask Museum, with 1,500 masks used in Indian and religious festivals from every part of Mexico, are standout attractions. It is a good overnight stop for travellers driving from the US to Mexico City.

The ghost town of **Real de Catorce**, an hour's drive to the north, was a boisterous mining community of 30,000 at the end of the 19th century. You can poke around its well preserved ruins, the empty shops, cantinas, a theatre, and cock-fighting arena. In these mountains Indians collect the hallucinogenic buttons of the *peyote* cactus, eaten to induce religious trances.

MORELIA AND MICHOACÁN

Sober **Morelia**, capital of the state of Michoacán, isn't a 'Silver City', but it is 180km (112 miles) south of Guanajuato and is conveniently visited on a tour of the mining towns. Michoacán's wealth comes from its lakes, forests and farmland, and it is famed as Mexico's fruit-growing state. The roads drop down sharply through rugged volcanic scenery from the highlands of Guanajuato to fertile plains. They run along or-

Colonial influences are much in evidence at this restaurant in Morelia.

chards and irrigated fields of alfalfa and strawberries where you can buy huge quantities of berries for next to nothing. In small towns such as **Comonfort**, you'll see a flag outside shops signalling freshly butchered meat, and big slabs of pork crackling called **chicharrón** being deep-fried in kettles of fat and hung up to dry. With a sprinkling of chile or lime juice, crunchy chicharrón makes a tempting snack. Roadside stands advertise **carnitas**, plates of fried or grilled bits of pork, and **cabrito al horno**, roast kid. Chunks of watermelon, papaya and pineapple are served in paper cones.

Morelia is austere and aristocratic. Its centre, the **Plaza de Armas**, could be a square in old Castille. The majestic cathedral is grey-stoned and the resonant tones of its great bells are solemn. The interior, too, has the classic sobriety of Spain. The colonists who founded the city in 1537 named it after Spain's Valladolid. It became Morelia in 1828 in honour of the independence leader Jose María Morelos, a *mestizo* priest born here. Around the 18th-century cathedral and partly arcaded square are palatial mansions, some converted as banks and hotels, but retaining their cloistered inner courtyards. The effect is a balanced, serene architectural harmony.

Papier-mâché masks are used to great effect during festivals.

Typical of the style is the **Palacio de Gobierno** on Avenida Francisco Madero. Once a seminary, its court and stone stairways are now decorated with murals of independence scenes. There are murals everywhere, lit up at night, providing the only bright colour in town. It's hard to tell the new from the old in Morelia because the city has been carefully preserved and reconstructed. Each building is topped with ornamental cornices, urns and wreaths, and cannon-shaped waterspouts drain flat roofs.

In the evening, there's lively conversation in the cafés under the arches, for this is a highly politicized university town. Political slogans, posters and graffiti cover the street walls. Michoacán was the stronghold of the reformer-President Lázaro Cárdenas and today of his son Cuauhtémoc's PRD party that challenges the establishment's party, the PRI.

Morelia is also a music centre. Sunday mass at the **Santa Rosa** church, west of the Plaza de Armas on Calle Negromante, is sometimes accompanied by the internationally famed **Niños Cantores de Morelia** choir from the adjoining Conservatory of Music. This was the first music school in the Americas, founded in 1590. Also on C. Negromante is the **Palacio Clavijero**, where the tourist office occupies a 17th-century Jesuit school attached to the baroque church of the same period across the street, now the public library.

Long Live the
Day of the Dead

Chocolate skulls, sugar skeletons, coffin cookies, bone-shaped bread. These are racked up by the millions for sale on 1st and 2nd November, when all Mexico observes the Día de los Muertos – the Day of the Dead. Far from being mournful, the holiday is a celebration, a time for visiting cemeteries and having picnics by the graves of departed relatives.

Food, tequila, cigarettes and sweets are prepared as an annual offering for the departed and are placed beside family altars in the home on 1st November, All Saint's Day. Later, or on the following day, All Soul's Day, the dishes may be eaten at home or taken to the graveside and consumed in a party atmosphere.

The native religions of Mexico regarded life and death as two sides of the same coin, as a continuum and equally acceptable parts of human experience. After the Conquest, Spanish fatalism and characteristic preoccupation with death, rooted as much in the deep Islamic influence in Spain as in medieval Catholicism, fitted neatly with the Mexican temperament.

*The **Tarascan** Indian celebration attracts tourists to Lake Pátzcuaro and Janitzio island. Tarascan communities carrying candles ring the lakeshore at night, communing with those who drowned. No fishing is done during this holiday.*

Behind the library, Morelia's speciality, candied fruit, is sold under the arches of the **Mercado de Dulces** on Calle Gómez Farías. On the south side of the main plaza, the **Museo Regional de Michoacán** on Calle Allende covers the state's history in art from early pre-Columbian clay figurines to colonial period religious paintings. Next door is the baroque **San Agustín** church whose open cloister becomes a food fair in the evenings, where cooks wave morsels from their grills to tempt customers. Another evening sight is the illuminated **Aqueduct** of 253 arches that runs for 1.5km right into town. The Tarascan fountain at the end of the aquaduct also becomes illuminated.

Three blocks east of the cathedral, an open-air market is held on the square in front of the **San Francisco** church. Its former cloister is now the Casa de las Artesanías del Estado, one of the best craft centres in Mexico. Here you'll find the top line of Michoacán's enchanting handicrafts. When you've visited two floors of exhibits you can buy many of the same products in the museum shop at fixed prices. There are earthenware jars big enough for Ali Baba's 40 thieves to hide in, beautiful green pottery with a spiky pineapple surface from San José de Gracia, lacquer boxes from Uruapan, brown pots with floral designs from Huacinto, carved wood furniture, embroidered blouses, Colima ceramic dancing dogs, decorated gourds, intricately incised and hammered copper vessels from Santa Clara del Cobre, masks, and textiles. You might see Indian women bringing in their wares to be sold. The museum and shop will give you a good idea of what to look for and how much to pay when you visit these villages and you might even see the artists at work. The centre is open from 10 a.m. to 8 p.m., closed on Monday.

From Morelia you can continue to Lake Pátzcuaro and on to Guadalajara or return to Mexico City. There are flights daily to the capital. The scenic trip by road can be made in under five hours. But wildlife lovers will want to make the detour to the **Monarch Butterfly Sanctuary** at Angangueo in the Sierra Madre Occidental. The turnoff on Highway 15 is at San Felipe de los Alzatl. From the village, a truck takes you over a rough road to a fir forest and an amazing sight. Every branch seems to sag under the gently fluttering orange and black wings of tens of millions of tightly packed monarch butterflies. They migrate every autumn from Canada and the American midwest and return in spring. The Sanctuary is open from 8 a.m. to 5 p.m., November through March. There is a small entrance. Highway 15 passes **Toluca**, capital of the State of Mexico. If it's Friday, be sure to visit the market, one of the largest and liveliest in the country. Toluca is only an hour by bus from Mexico City and makes a pleasant outing.

LAKE PÁTZCUARO

The Tarascan Indians of Michoacán were never defeated, neither by the Aztecs nor by the Spaniards, though they submitted peacefully when they saw what Cortés did to Tenochtitlán. They were themselves brutally treated by the infamous conquistador Nuño de Guzmán. These hardy Indians speak Purépecha, unrelated to any other tongue in Mexico. They were the first to master metallurgy, working copper for spear points and vessels. Some authorities claim the Tarascans had links with metalworking peoples of South America.

The heart of their domain is beautiful **Lake Pátzcuaro**. Green volcanic mountains ring the lake and promontories reach out to its three islands. **Janitzio Island** rises steeply to a monumental statue of Morelos, raising a clenched fist skyward. Morelos is always portrayed with the scarf he wrapped around his forehead to ease his chronic migraines. Boats run out to the island every 20 minutes or so from El Muelle, on the outskirts of Pátzcuaro town. The dock of El Muelle is lined with stalls and cafés where the lake's small white fish are deep-fried and served up by the platter or wrapped in a tortilla.

The fishermen of Janitzio used to go out in canoes in the morning mists with curious butterfly-shaped nets, a favourite shot for photographers. Nowadays, deforestation and the resulting runoff of silt into the lake, along with the use of fertilizers in

161

Morning sun rises over Lake Pátzcuaro.

nearby fields, have polluted the waters and fed rampant water hyacinth growth. The plant is choking the lake and fishing is in trouble – the nets have all but disappeared.

Handicrafts flourish thanks to a Spanish priest, Don Vasco de Quiroga, who founded **La Compañía** church and one of the first schools for Indians in Pátzcuaro in 1540. 'Tata Vasco', as the Tarascans fondly call him, encouraged each village to specialize in a different craft, as they do to this day. He made Pátzcuaro both the provincial capital and his See when appointed bishop.

The town was graced with noble mansions and fat pillared arches on its main square. But when Vasco de Quiroga died, the capital of Michoacán was moved to Morelia, leaving Pátzcuaro to acquire the attractive patina of age with few modern changes. On a smaller square, the **Plaza Gertrudis Bocanegra,** is the apse of a church converted to the town library; it holds a noteworthy mural of Tarascan tribulations by **Juan O'Gorman**.

Pátzcuaro's justly famous market fronts on this square and recedes into a labyrinth of alleys, sheds and stalls. You'll see blue tortillas made of Indian maize along with other goods and handicrafts from the region being sold for native use. You can watch artisans at work on lacquer boxes and embroidery in the **Casa de los Once Patios**, a state workshop. It is a block from the central plaza, on Calle Lerín. More crafts are displayed in the excellent small **Museo de Artes Populares**, one block north at C. Quiroga. (Open from 9 a.m. to 7 p.m., except on Mondays; closed at 3 p.m. on Sunday.) The building was originally Tata Vasco's school, the **Colegio de San Nicolás**.

In villages all around the lake virtually every house is a workshop. **Santa Clara del Cobre** fairly dazzles with shining copper. The region's renowned inlaid gold lacquerware comes from **Quiroga**; **Tocuaro** is famous for its masks; **San Jerónimo Purenchécuaro** for embroidery and figures made from straw and reeds; **Jarácuaro** for straw hats; **San José de Gracia** for its unique bristle-surfaced dark green pottery; and **Ocumicho** for grotesque animal figurines. The best Mexican guitars are made in **Paracho**.

The Tarascan capital had the sibiliant name Tzintzuntzan, (pronounced *sin-SOON-san*), meaning 'Place of the Hummingbird'. The ruins are right on the Morelia road and overlook the lake. Not much has survived except large platforms that once held temples. From Pátzcuaro a scenic mountain drive of about an hour brings you down to the avocado orchards of **Uruapan**. The

Papier-mâché figures are a part of the Día de los Muertos (Day of the Dead) celebrations.

town is also famous for its handpainted lacquerware. Uruapan is the ideal base for visiting the nowdormant baby volcano **El Paracutín**. One day in 1943 a cornfield began to bubble and smoke. When it stopped nine years later, a 600m (2,000ft) cone covered the cornfield and a number of surrounding villages. You can see the tower of a church poking through the black lava field. Horses can be rented at Angahuan to visit the moonscape scene. Uruapan's lacquerware has floral designs on boxes and trays – perhaps inspired by the tranquil floral landscape now protected as **Eduardo Ruiz National** Park, extending from the city limits to the Cupatitzio River and its waterfalls.

163

Above: Festival day at Ocumicho, Michoacán.

Below: the crater of El Paracutín volcano.

GUADALAJARA AND THE PACIFIC RESORTS

GUADALAJARA AND LAKE CHAPALA

The *Tapatios*, as residents of the state of Jalisco are nicknamed, call their beloved capital, **Guadalajara**, 'The City of Roses'. It's a modern metropolis sprawling over a sloping plain at a comfortable 1,550m (5,000ft). With more than 4 million people, it is Mexico's second biggest city. To get at Guadalajara's special treasures, save time and energy by taking the inexpensive taxis and horse-drawn **calandrias**.

A good starting point is the colonial district around the **Cathedral**, a landmark seen from afar. Begun in 1558 when northwestern Mexico was called Nueva Galicia, this imposing church is a blend of many styles, including rather 'un-Mexican' Gothic spires covered in bright yellow tile erected after an earthquake in 1848. Four spacious plazas that

open the heart of the city for strolling flank the Cathedral. The front faces west on the **Plaza de los Laureles** and its fountain; the north on the **Rotonda** where revolutionary heroes are buried. The church is backed by the **Plaza de la Liberación**, a modern square with underground parking.

The classic **Teatro Degollado** and **Museo Regional de Guadalajara** face this square. Check the theatre for concert schedules and performances of the local folkloric ballet. The museum's collection of perky ceramic dogs from Colima and big-nosed Nayarit figurines is one of the country's most complete. Note the section on *charros*, the fancy-dress gentlemen cowboys – an extravagant *charro* costume is worn by Mariachis. Jalisco is the epicentre of both these Mexican traditions. South, the **Plaza de Armas** and its amusingly elaborate bandstand are dominated by the 18th-century **Palacio de Gobierno**. The central staircase provides a dramatic setting for José Clemente Orozco's mural masterpiece of Father Hidalgo, arms flung wide, proclaiming independence. Other panels in Orozco's violent imagery lampoon religion and depict the horrors of war.

The **Plaza Tapatía**, a modern tree-shaded pedestrian mall of shops and restaurants, leads from the Teatro Degollado to the **Hospicio Cabañas**. This former orphanage houses a cultural centre. Its chapel walls are completely covered by

powerful black and grey Orozco murals expressing the artist's pain at man's cruelty to man. A mirror is provided so you can examine without neck strain the blazing colours of his 'Man of Fire' painting in the cupola overhead. (More of his best work, done between 1935 and 1939, is in the auditorium of the **University** on Avenida Juárez.) Around the corner from the Hospicio, the huge two-storey **Mercado Libertad** is the city's boisterous central market. Leather goods are a speciality here, particularly the *huarache* sandals of woven thongs. You might be tempted to try on a broad-brimmed embroidered *charro* sombrero. A better choice of the state's handicrafts is offered at the **Casa de las Artesanías de Jalisco** in the large **Agua Azul Park**, a taxi ride south on the Calzada Independencia.

Beyond the market, just off Independencia, a staccato blare of trumpets will guide you to the café-lined **Plazuela de los Mariachis**. For the equivalent of a few dollars, you can sip the speciality of the nearby town of Tequila and be serenaded at the very source of mariachi music. The little square echoes with repeated renditions of *Guadalajara* all day, but evening is when it really jumps.

Ixtlán, in Guadalajara, boasts a natural geyser of impressive size.

To hear this music at its best, take a 20-minute taxi ride to the suburb of **San Pedro Tlaquepaque** and its enclosed plaza, **El Parián**. The village streets have blossomed with fashionable boutiques and this is the place to go for Guadalajara blown glass, ceramics and other crafts. Another village swallowed by the city, **Tonalá**, a bit farther east, is where those smooth-finished ceramic animals decorated with floral patterns are made, Tonalá's market days are Tuesday and Sunday.

The best time to visit Guadalajara's flea market, **El Baratillo**, is on Sunday morning; it's located on Calle 38 and Javier Mina. Follow this with a display of daredevil horsemanship and bulldozing at the **Lienzo Charro** in Agua Azul Park. Bullfights are held from December to April in the **Plaza Monumental**.

The largest colony of North Americans ouside the US and Canada, an estimated 30,000, have settled in Guadalajara and its environs. A year-round spring climate and the low cost of living are the main attractions, not to mention the natural beauty of **Lake Chapala**, the home-away-from-home for many retirees. The lake is Mexico's largest, 83km (52 miles) long. **Chapala**, **Ajijic** (*ah-hee-HEEK*) and **Jocotepec** (*ho-KO-tepec*) are artsy-craftsy communities the expatriates have made their own. There are three golf clubs open to visitors in the Guadalajara-Chapala area.

PACIFIC BEACHES

Some of Mexico's finest Pacific beaches are on the **Costa de Oro** (Gold Coast), west of Guadalajara, and travelling between them covers some spectacular tropical scenery. When beachcombers want a change, they can always slip on their shoes and get over to Guadalajara, just a hop away, for shopping and a bit of city life.

Manzanillo

Manzanillo, at the southern end of the Costa de Oro, has been around a long time. The harbour beneath the knob of the Cerro de la Cruz (Hill of the Cross) was used for shipbuilding and the Pacific trade in the 16th century. The string of beaches northward where mountains come down to the sea have had a steady winter clientele who like the small, comfortable hotels, whilst there is also much to explore in the countryside. But it was the construction of a dream-resort complex, **Las Hadas** ('the Fairies'), by the Bolivian tin multimillionaire Antinor Patiño, that put Manzanillo on the jet-set map.

Las Hadas stands on a promontory over Santiago Bay, a dream out of the Arabian Nights. The fairyland effect is strongest at night, when the whole hillside is floodlit. Las Hadas has spawned construction up and down the adjoining beaches; there are golf clubs, condominiums and villas, a strip of hotels, bars and restaurants.

The town of Manzanillo is undistinguished, except for delicious fresh shrimp and fish brought in from the working port. A sailfish tournament is held in November and charter boats go out for other big game fish all year round. Shops seem overloaded with novelty T-shirts and curios made from shells, such as a truly curious Christ crucified on three clams. **Las Brisas** beach, closest to town, is broad and uncrowded. It leads to **Playa Azul**, **Las Hadas**, **Playa Santiago** and a succession of sheltered coves. Pelicans and frigate birds, soaring champions of the Pacific, are endlessly fascinating as they patrol the shore.

An event of the day may be watching fishermen slowly close a circle of nets offshore, then pull them on to the beach, with everyone helping haul the lines until the silvery catch is flopping on the sand. South of Manzanillo in April and May, the 'Green Wave', a monster swell 10m (30ft) high, occasionally rolls in from the Pacific.

Through the avocado and mango orchards on the road north you'll catch a glimpse of sandy beaches. This coast, one guesses, is destined for development, but for the time being it is largely unspoiled. By car or by boat, one can reach isolated coves. **Barra de Navidad**, another 16th-century Spanish base for Asian exploration, and **San Patricio-Melaque** are at opposite ends of a 5km (3-mile) beach backed by a lagoon. Both little towns have a lan-

guid atmosphere and inexpensive accommodation A favourite programme is to walk the beach one way, savour some seafood at an outdoor restaurant, and take a shuttle bus back. A big hotel has most of lovely **Tecatita Bay** to itself, and there are campsites on beaches fringed with coco palms down side roads all along the coast. The road rises and falls, twists and turns as it crosses ridge after jungle ridge, sloping steeply westward like the backs of great green animals leaning down to drink from the sea. The loveliest section is the **Costa Careyes**, 120km (75 miles) north of Manzanillo. The few hotels and lavish villas scattered on the hillsides above a chain of little coves enjoy privacy and unparalleled views.

Puerto Vallarta

Puerto Vallarta, or P.V. as regulars call it, is the most popular Pacific Coast resort after Acapulco. Though it is a fraction the size of that city and still has a village feel to it, the tall hotels are rising north and south of town on Bahía de Banderas, a crescent bay 100km (62 miles) across. From high green mountains

169

Maguey Spirits

Chances are that you'll be introduced to tequila before you even check into your hotel. Hostesses with pitchers of margaritas circulate in airports and hotel lobbies to welcome the thirsty tourists and hook them on Mexico's national tipple. It is deceptively mild and refreshing, but packs a wicked punch.

Tequila is made by fermenting juice extracted from the heart of the blue maguey plant. This is not a cactus, but an agave, a relative of the century plant. A cluster of thick leaves a couple of metres long rise from the ground around a tall spike with flowers at the top when in bloom. In the centre of the flower, like the heart of an artichoke, is the pineapple-shaped core, the piña, which is cut out, roasted and squeezed to extract juice which, when fermented and aged, becomes tequila. True tequila, the real stuff, is limited by government regulation to liquor produced in the provinces around Guadalajara.

The margarita is always served in a salt-rimmed glass. This makes a happy contrast with the tart concoction of fresh lime juice, sweet orange-based liqueur and tequila, briskly shaken to a froth with ice.

Mezcal *is a speciality of the Oaxaca region. It is made from the juice of other maguey plants and has a different flavour from tequila, as you can verify at the many mezcal distilleries and shops along the road and in the towns between Oaxaca and Mitla. Some of the best bottled mezcal contains a maguey worm (gusano) pickled in booze at the bottom of the bottle and has a little sack of mixed salt, chile powder and a dried, ground maguey worm attached to the bottle.*

Both tequila and mezcal are slightly less alcoholic (around 76 proof) than whisky or gin. When aged, these liquors may be labelled 'añejo' or 'viejo', and will have a golden colour.

They are often taken neat in a shot glass after licking some salt (or the salt-chile-worm mixture) off your fist. There's a ritual that goes along with it: raise the glass and say 'arriba', lower it saying 'abajo', bring it up to your chest with 'al centro', and down it in one gulp after finishing with 'aden-tro'. ('Up, down, to the middle and inside.') Salud! (To your health!) is good enough thereafter.

Pulque *is the poor man's drink in the countryside and in pulquerías, fairly raunchy cantinas in working-class urban neighbourhoods. You can't order pulque in ordinary restaurants or bars. It is also made from maguey juice, but is fermented, not distilled, and is much less alcoholic. It is slightly thick, white and sweetish and should be consumed as fresh as possible. Sometimes it is served curado, with a fruit flavouring.*

Lizzarding in the sun takes on a new meaning at Puerto Vallarta.

ringing the bay, rivers spill down jungle waterfalls and empty into the sea. Cool mountain breezes keep the sunny days comfortable. The tennis rackets *thwack* on countless courts, parasailers float over the beach, donkey polo matches with brooms for mallets kick up the sand, and speed boats zoom back and forth.

In P.V. the beach has become a stage and most of the swimming and sunning goes on at hotel pools. Where the hotel's concrete meets the beach there's a neutral trading zone under the palm trees – tourists and beach vendors do a brisk business in straw hats, silver jewellery and *serapes*. When the sun sets behind Cabo Corrientes, everything stops for the spectacle of gold and crimson fading to rose and purple in the sky. About the same time, the margarita mixers begin to whir faster for the hours formally declared to be 'Happy'. Along the Malecón, the seaside esplanade in town, the traditional *paseo*, or evening stroll, draws clusters of young and old in the twilight. And as the hour grows late, music throbs through the night, and out on the bay, moonlight 'booze cruises' sail by. Forecast for the morrow? 'Clear and Sunny ...'

Sooner or later, everyone takes a cab or minibus to **Mismaloya**, a few miles south of town around a promontory. The little bay is getting more than its share of development, but there are still thatched *palapas* where you can eat fresh shrimp and fish grilled on sticks over an open

fire, while the green water laps at your feet and pelicans waddle around, awaiting scraps. You can still climb up the ridge to the ruins of the set built for the film *Night of the Iguana*.

Ava Gardner played opposite Richard Burton in John Huston's film, but it was the romance between Burton and Elizabeth Taylor that got the headlines and started the Hollywood Vallarta vogue. There's even a rather gruesome waxy-looking statue to the pair. It's just beyond a bridge over the Cuale River, which divides the town. The stream bed, nearly dry in winter, is called Gringo Gulch because many North Americans have their homes along its banks, as Liz and Richard did. About two kilometres inland, you come across Eden de Mismaloya,

An hotel swimming pool in Puerto Vallarta.

through the centre on Highway 200 with a deafening clatter. A refreshing, shady retreat is an island found between bridges on the river. Birds twitter, men read the papers over a cup of coffee, and a little girl plays with an iguana outside a shop that sells the same reptiles stuffed. Adjoining the upper bridge, the town market has a range of handicrafts on sale.

Cruise ships and sport-fishing boats dock at the marina north of town. A ferry used to link P.V. with Cabo San Lucas overnight. It may be in service again one day; meanwhile, there are daily flights to Baja destinations, as well as to US cities.

From the marina, sailboats cruise down the coast to **Yalapa**, an isolated beach on the jungle edge, accessible only by sea. The bigger hotels and the bullring are out this way and construction creeping north will before long join **Nueva Vallarta**, a resort on the Nayarit State side of the bay. Nayarit is on Mountain Standard Time, so set your watch back an hour when you cross the Ameca River border. The Los Flamingos golf course is off this road.

Further out, numerous relatively undeveloped beaches are in easy reach by car. The favourite rental

which served as the location for another film, *Predator*.

The white houses and cobbled streets of downtown P.V. are densely packed with restaurants, bars, boutiques, jewellery shops and handicraft studios. Some of the biggest names in resort fashions are represented, along with booths selling tickets for riding or a sail, or the lottery. Buses and trucks roar

173

model is an open Volkswagen Beetle with most of the body stripped away. Traditional Mexican farming life goes its unhurried way just a few kilometres out of Puerto Vallarta, up steep mountain roads where views can be superb and well worth the extra drive.

Ixtapa-Zihuatanejo

When Puerto Vallarta began to become a household word, the avant-garde of beachcombing discovered **Zihuatanejo** (pronounced *see-wah-ta-NAY-ho*), a tiny fishing village between Manzanillo and Acapulco. It had what they wanted: a sparkling bay divided into intimate beaches by outcroppings of rock and wooded knolls, the simple pleasures of swimming and sunning, and the freshest of fruit and seafood, not to mention cheap beer and rum.

The secret didn't last long. FONATUR, the government agency that created Cancún, picked the area for its next venture, **Ixtapa** (*ees-TAH-pa*). Now the pair, only 9.5km (6 miles) apart but separated by the terrain, make an admirable parlay: Zihuatanejo for the charm of a village and its necklace of beaches, Ixtapa for manicured luxury on its own long beach, a good golf course, tennis, windsurfing and all the amenities of a top resort, without the

traffic and hustle of an Acapulco. Its hotels are ultra-modern, designed to fit harmoniously into the tropical environment. Minibuses shuttle back and forth between the two, or you can rent a moped for independence.

Zihuatanejo has grown more sophisticated, with boutiques and candle-lit restaurants overlooking the bay, but fishermen still bring in their catch at the town dock. From there, you can take a boat out to the rocky point at **Las Gatas** – ideal for snorkelling and diving – or to the secluded beaches of Ixtapa Island.

A peaceful lagoon wakes up to the rising sun.

Further North

The road to Guadalajara, 340km (211 miles) away, turns off up the coast at Compostela. Northward, **San Blas** is yet another 16th-century port that served the Manila trade. The old customs house is a relic of its past. Fray Junípero Serra sailed from here in 1768 to begin his life's work, founding the missions of California. There's terrific surfing at **Matanchen** just south of town, and a string of other pleasant beaches and coves, as well as bird-watching and mosquito slapping in the mangrove lagoons and rainforest behind the shore. The rainy season on the coast is from May to September, but rainfall is usually limited to afternoon showers.

The coast north is becoming developed in spots. **Mazatlán** has long been famed for billfish sport and as the shrimp capital of the universe, with **Guaymas** running a close second. Both have long-established clubs and modern hotels on their beaches. The new resorts are being built on the **Sea** of **Cortés**, where the air is dry, rainfall is measured in millimetres and the landscape resembles Baja California.

BAJA AND THE NORTH

on gorgeous beaches and more are a-building, with golf and tennis now added to the superb fishing and water sports. With all these facilities, Baja is still peaceful and unhurried and the beaches are empty for kilometre upon kilometre – a paradise for holiday makers.

Out on a limb of the continent, 'Baja' (*Ba-ha*) began its tourist life as a fisherman's secret, a place where Hollywood stars like John Wayne came in their private planes or yachts for fabulous catches of marlin and sailfish.

Today, the secret is out – Baja is booming. A 1,160km (726-mile) highway skirting the peninsula's arid mountainous spine connects Tijuana in the north to the southern tip at Cabo San Lucas, linking the few important towns and crossing the Tropic of Cancer on the way. (Every two years a band of maniacal drivers does it the hard way in the gruelling 24-hour, 1,000-mile 'Baja Mil' off-the-road race.) Airlines fly in from Alaska, Canada and US cities. Resort hotels and condos are in place

A panoramic view of the 'Barranca del Cobre' (Copper Canyon) – a breath-taking natural phenomenon.

BAJA SOUTH

Cabo San Lucas, the original fishing port, and **San José del Cabo**, more recently developed by the government's FONATUR agency for tourism, are jointly called **Los Cabos** ('the Capes'). A spectacular stretch of coast runs for 32km (20 miles) between the two. Flying in, you'll see this is cactus country – more than 100 varieties are found in Mexico, from tiny buttons to *saguaros* 15m (50ft) tall and the weird, looping *'boojum'*, found only on the peninsula. As if there

weren't enough in the wild, Baja nurseries supply cactus plants for local landscaping and cactus gardens.

In San José del Cabo the hotel zone is set apart from the town, right on the beach, and so far, the hotels are widely separated, with plenty of privacy. The blissful quietude – a luxury in boisterous Mexico – is broken only by the pounding of the surf and the cries of sea birds. Beach vendors and speed boats haven't arrived ... yet. (There are six times as many people in Acapulco as in the entire state of Baja California Sur.)

You can do your own off-the-road exploration in a 'Baja Buggy', the topless stripped-down Volkswagens made in Mexico. San José's golf course is a green oasis in the desert, with angular peaks of brown mountains rising some 1,800m (6,000ft) as a backdrop. Lack of humidity in the air sharply etches every detail miles away, and this dryness keeps you comfortable even when temperatures climb to 30°C (90°F) and over at midday.

At Cabo San Lucas you'll be besieged by boat captains. There are at least a hundred varying kinds of craft for rent, from around $85 per person for four sharing a power cruiser to half that price for a *panga*, a motorized skiff, including equipment and fishing license. The deep-sea fishermen come back around lunchtime. Rare is the boat that doesn't fly at least one marlin pennant and there's almost always a big fish being hung up on the dock to be weighed and

Big Greys of Baja

For whale-watching, Baja California is unsurpassed. Every winter in December and January, some 15,000 California Grey whales arrive along the coast at the end of a 8,300km (5,000-mile) migration from the north. The females come to give birth and teach their calves how to come up for air in the warm, shallow waters of Baja lagoons. The Greys are up to 18m (60ft) long and may weigh 100 tonnes. The calves are 4.5m (15ft) long at birth. By March, after fattening on 190 litres of milk a day, the calves are ready to make the long trip back north.

*The main calving grounds are at **Laguna Ojo de Liebre**, also known as Scammon's Lagoon, about halfway up the peninsula, not an easy place to get to. Scammon was an American whaler who started the slaughter of the Greys that reduced their number to about 300 at the turn of the century. Now protected, they have made a strong comeback. You can see whales spouting and sounding in the open sea from Los Cabos. Or you can take a whale-watch boat tour from the marina. Boats sometimes come so close that you'll get a splashing from the flukes of diving whales.*

photographed with its captor. They can run over 1,000lb, and 250-pounders are routine. To conserve the species, no boat is allowed to bring in more than two. Others caught must be released, though after putting up a fight for an hour and being gaffed, many of these do not survive for long.

They call these fishing grounds 'Marlin Alley', but there are an incredible 857 species of fish in the area. You'll see scores of varieties on the ten-minute glass-bottom boat ride from the marina that takes you out to **Los Arcos**, where the blue Pacific slams into spray against pillars of granite as it mingles with the turquoise of the Sea of Cortés. There's a sand strip under eroded cliffs called 'Lover's Beach' here at Baja's end. You can snorkel in 30-degree water around the rocks where sea lions doze and pelicans perch. Climb up a bit and scan the sea: a whirl of white water marks big fish chasing little ones. A marlin jumping seems to stand on his tail.

Scuba divers come to San Lucas to witness the phenomenon of the **Cascadas de Arena**, an underwater sandfall carried by currents to a point where it pours in a stream over the edge of a trench 270m (900ft) deep. Diving gear and lessons are available at the marina, and the *pangas* can take you out to diving and fishing sites. With luck, from December to March you might glide into a pod of whales.

La Paz, on the Sea of Cortés, is served by international airlines and is a short hop from Los Cabos. Or you can take a four-hour bus ride through starkly barren mountains where buzzards ride the thermals above deep canyons. La Paz was once famed for its pearl fishing, described in John Steinbeck's novel *The Pearl*. But the oysters died out fifty years ago and La Paz slumbered in the sun until the current Baja boom brought tourism. Some of the best diving and snorkelling is off the secluded beaches of Espíritu Santo island, a picnic day's sail from Pichilingue harbour where the ferries from the mainland dock.

La Paz claims to have the most sensational sunsets in the world – the sea turns shades of red, and streaks of cloud ignite into flames as the sun disappears behind the dark purple bar across the bay. Patches of bright blue sky set off the livid clouds. The skyscape keeps changing until your film runs out, and then it gets even better.

Baja defeated Cortés. He landed here in 1535 and later tried to implant a settlement, but this wasn't accomplished until a Franciscan mission was founded at **Loreto** in 1697. This was the first of a chain that was established nearly a century later up the coast in Alta California – as the present US state was called under Mexican rule. Now the Californians are coming back south and FONATUR has paved the way with an airport and deluxe hotels on sparkling Nopolo Bay, where the sun never takes a holiday and annual rainfall is almost nil. The Sea of Cortés is a cul-de-sac, a natural trap for fish that swim in at the southern end and take a while to find their way back out. In Loreto, August is the best month for marlin and sailfish. Whales come into the Sea of Cortés, too. In addition to billfish, fishermen take record catches of yellow fin tuna, wahoo and dorado at both La Paz and Loreto.

BAJA NORTH

Tijuana used to be called 'Sin City', but many a sin has been legalized since the bad old days of US Prohibition, and 'T.J.' today shapes up more as 'Sale City', if tourist statistics are a measure. Tijuana is the foreign city most visited by Americans and most go over to shop. They say that more traffic passes under the Freedom Arch at the California border than at any other crossing in the world: some 40 million trips a year. It's so easy – border police are there to speed up in-bound traffic, not to look at documents. Not even a Tourist Card is required if you're staying less than four days and not going farther than Ensenada. All of Baja California is a duty-free zone, so there are bargains on liquor and imported luxuries, plus incredible trash that somebody must buy or it wouldn't be there. The full range of Mexico's colourful crafts is on sale here too, in the government's Centro Artesanal and in shops along Av. Revolución or in the modern shopping mall in the Río Tijuana section. It is pretty frantic at times.

Not as frantic as in the 20s perhaps, when the Hollywood crowd and half the US Navy from San Pedro-San Diego used to line up at 'the longest bar in the world'. But there are still superlatives, the margaritas come in pitchers, the food at countless restaurants is authentically Mexican and the nightclubs are as raunchy as you can get. There's plenty of sporting life out at the Agua Caliente **Hipódromo** track on weekends, where *galgos* (greyhounds) take over from the horses at night-racing, and at lightning fast *jai-alai* games in the **Frontón Palacio**. Bullfights are scheduled every Sunday in summer in two rings.

The face of the new, commercial Tijuana, the fourth largest city in Mexico, is presented by the fast-growing factories where low-cost Mexican labour assembles electronic products, and by the lively Cultural Centre on the river where there's always a fiesta of Mexican music and dance. But you don't have to look far to find the old face of Sin City still leering underneath the cosmetic clean-up.

The tollway south, Mexico 1, quickly brings you to more sedate **Ensenada**, the long-established resort and fishing town on Todos Santos Bay, also Baja's busiest port. The drive down the cliff-lined coast is exhilarating and you can stop to look for migrating whales, navigating along the shore in December and January. In summer, watch the

surfers. East of Tijuana is a rich agricultural area and the state's capital, **Mexicali** and its California counterpart, Caléxico. The border crossing there leads to **San Felipe** at the top of the Sea of Cortés. Tides here drop 10m (30ft), compared to 1m (3ft) at Los Cabos. It's a weekend hangout for dune-buggy stunt drivers.

✓ **COPPER CANYON**

Copper Canyon is one face of Mexico most visitors never see, but those who do, never forget. The trip on the Chihuahua-Pacific Railroad from Los Mochis in Sinaloa on the eastern shore of the Sea of Cortés winds through the heart of the Sierra Madre Occidental and down to the plains of Chihuahua. The single-track line climbs 2,456m (8,000ft) to

Faint-hearted abstain! Drinks in Mexico come in generous measures.

the rim of Copper Canyon, a wilderness gorge bigger than the Grand Canyon. On the way the track goes through 86 tunnels and over 39 bridges, an engineering feat begun in 1898 by an American entrepreneur as part of his dream of linking Kansas City to the Pacific Ocean. Sixty-three years and $100 million later it was completed by the Mexican government.

The train makes the 672km (420-mile) trip in under 13 hours, including a stop at **Divisadero**, allowing passengers to look down into the canyon and to buy trinkets from the Tarahumara Indians.

181

The high country is heavily forested with pines. You'll see waterfalls, log cabins and logging camps, and pink, buff and grey rim rock like the ramparts of walled cities. Strange formations resemble spired cathedrals and towers. Prankish giants seem to have left huge boulders balanced precariously on top of each other.

The canyon as seen from Divisadero is actually the junction of three gorges more than 1,200m (4,000ft) deep. This is the hideout of the **Tarahumaras**, who evaded civilization until the 20th century.

With binoculars you can see where they live in caves and shelters built in the cliffs. Now they're complaining that drug operators have invaded their remote tribal lands to grow marijuana. The Tarahumara are famed for their ability to run for days. At stations along the way,

the women sell food, dolls, neatly carved violins and beautiful baskets. A peculiar local souvenir are the stuffed and varnished frogs posed playing a guitar.

There are several good lodges near the canyon. You can stay overnight, walk along the canyon rim or even arrange the eight-hour trip to the bottom. A freight train carries campers, cars and trailers over the continental divide, connecting with the ferry to Baja at Los Mochis, or with the coast road to Mazatlán. The lodges have fireplaces, and a warm sweater will be welcome on frosty winter mornings.

On the Chihuahua side, the cattle ranches, grain fields and fruit orchards of Mexico's biggest state sprawl across a prairie where abrupt, bare mountains thrust up like islands in a vast dry sea bed. At Cuauhtémoc the train passes the neat farms of a German Mennonite community, famous in Mexico for its cheeses. No TV antennas here: the Mennonites forbid modern contraptions. Houses and towns are few and far between. Sometimes a horse-drawn buckboard will race the train, while cowboys wave their straw hats. Long stretches of empty highway under the big sky begin to give you an idea of the immense distances in Mexico.

Silhouettes of twisted and distorted cacti against the setting sun of the Chihuaha plains.

CHIHUAHUA

Chihuahua is a busy, clean city of 1.5 million, a five-hour drive south of El Paso, Texas. It was General Pancho Villa's headquarters and the house where his widow, Doña Luz, lived until 1981 is now the **Museo de la Revolución**. You can join the queues of note-taking school children to see the bullet-riddled 1922 open Dodge sedan in which Villa was ambushed in 1923. The museum has interesting photos of Pancho and his Dorados – Golden Boys – wrapped to the ears in cartridge belts. Villa's grave is in Chihuahua, but it's empty. When he was reburied in the Revolution Monument in Mexico City, his body was found without a head – no one knows why.

The national hero Father Hidalgo was imprisoned and then executed at a spot where the State Capitol now stands. A small museum and shop of Tarahumara crafts is at Av. Leyes de la Reforma 5. The Indians come to work on construction jobs in the city – you can spot them by their long hair and short stature. From Chihuahua it's an hour's flight to **Monterrey**, the industrial capital and third largest city in Mexico, and then another hour to Mexico City.

El Tajín, on the Gulf Coast – a dance in honour of the sun.

184

THE GULF COAST

 VERACRUZ

Veracruz isn't on most tourist itineraries. It is unaffected, unbuttoned, and very sure of itself. It has a good time and will make room for visitors to share the fun, but doesn't make a big business of it. Veracruz has the best Carnival and maybe the worst handicraft market. It is steeped in history, but has few monuments. It was here that Cortés landed and burned his boats, and here that Spanish dominion in Mexico ended three centuries later. The gold and silver galleons sailed for Spain from Veracruz, so it was a prime target for pirates. American marines and French *zouaves* invaded too. Today, as Mexico's principal seaport, the harbour is always filled with ships and the tooting of tugboats.

This is the background to keep in mind in Veracruz, but once you're there, the atmosphere will take over: just *being* there becomes more important than *doing* something. A lot of time can be passed happily just sit-ting in a café, listening to the special beat of local music, and imagining Humphrey Bogart, unshaven and in a stained white linen, making a deal with a shifty-eyed Peter Lorre at the next table. It's the archtypal tropical port you've seen in a hundred movies.

A look at the city could begin with a walk along the harbourside boulevard, the Malecón, which actually has several names as it winds past jetties and naval training schools. The naval cadets in their white uniforms give the squares a musical comedy air. A Stalinesque statue of President Venustiano Carranza, who briefly made Veracruz the capital of Mexico in 1914, presides over a plaza where they parade, his back to a former lighthouse and museum of the Carranza period. On the Malecón's broad esplanade tickets are sold for the boat ride out to the **Isla Sacrificios**, the lighthouse island where some remains of sacrifices were found. The short trip gives a breezy view of the city from the sea.

The **Mercado de Curiosidades** begins on this esplanade and turns the corner on to Calle Landero y Coss toward the Customs House. It is rightfully called the market of curios, for the crafts tend to tacky nicknacks made of sea shells, cheap scarves and plastic ship models. Across the street, on the Insurgentes section of the Malecón, ceiling fans stir the air in a block-long café as big and barren as a bus station. It is an

The Carnival at Veracruz is a major event.

institution, packed to overflowing at meal-times. Waiters circulating with a kettle in each hand pour thick black coffee into glasses, then let streams of hot foaming milk cascade from a height. Kids scoot around the tables like hockey players, while groups of matrons tucking into ice creams and pastries try to gossip over the din.

The **Museo Regional** at 397 Calle Zaragoza is worth visiting to sort out the turbulent history of the town. This is the only museum that documents the role of African slaves in Mexico. Cortés imported the first from Cape Verde to work his sugar plantations and in 1641 records showed 35,089 Negroes in New Spain. Communities founded by escaped slaves near Acapulco still have a strong African strain and the Cuban-African influence in music and race is marked around Veracruz. A pronouncement abolishing slavery was one of the first acts of Father Hidalgo during the uprising of 1810, but slaves were not actually freed until the constitution of 1857.

The museum also has a section of photos and costumes of Carnival, the main event of the year for *Jarochos*, as the people of Veracruz are called. Hotel reservations have to be made well in advance for this carousal. It begins on the Tuesday before Ash Wednesday in the zócalo with the burning of the effigy of *Mal Humor* (dull care) and ends with the symbolic burial of 'Juan Carnival', accompanied by a morality play on the evils of drink and infidelity. Clubs work all year long on their costumes, bands and floats for parades.

Another small and skippable museum is installed in the **Baluarte de Santiago**, a remnant of the once formidable but ineffectual city battlements. In front of the Customs House, note the 'Gracias México, 1939–1989' plaque placed here in the name of the 33,000 Republicans from the Spanish Civil War who found refuge in Mexico.

The heart of Veracruz is the **Plaza de Armas**, small as zócalos go, but throbbing with action. A dozen or so café-bars crowd their tables under the white arches of one side, closed to traffic. When the municipal band strikes up at 8 p.m. in front of the Moorish City Hall, half a dozen competing musical groups cut loose around the café tables.

The cafés open for breakfast, get into gear by mid-morning snack time, and really roll during the lunch hour that lasts from 2 to 5 p.m. What joy to confront a huge platter of fresh fat shrimp in their shells, with heaped lime quarters and two kinds of mayonnaise! How agreeable to have a bowl of lime-scented water and a fresh napkin brought to rinse your fingers! What bliss to have the waiter present a glistening fish for your inspection before having it grilled to perfection! How satisfying to top it off with strong, black Veracruz coffee and brandy! Service here is

San Juan de Ulúa Fortress

The most interesting historical monument in Veracruz lies across the harbour. You can ride out by boat from the Malecón, or take a bus from the Customs House to this sombre relic, now surrounded by the cranes and tracks of a container-ship dock and rail terminal. Built in the mid-18th century on the site of 16th-century fortifications, the bastion was the last Spanish foothold in Mexico. The Spanish fleet bombarded independence forces in Veracruz in 1822, when royalist refugees filled the fort. It finally surrendered to a young Mexican officer named Santa Anna making his first mark on history.

The fortress and its predecessors seem to have done little to protect Veracruz. The English privateers Sir Francis Drake and John Hawkins took and retook the city in the late 1500s, and Dutch freebooter Laurent de Graff, feared around the Gulf as 'Lorencillo', sacked and burned it for three days in 1683. The French bombarded the city twice, and the US three times, in 1847, 1914 and 1917. Small wonder that few monuments are left.

In the 19th century San Juan de Ulúa was a notoriously horrible prison, with walls 2.5m (8ft) thick and the sea for a moat. Carranza turned the prison headquarters into a presidential residence, but was assassinated before he could occupy it.

not measured as a percentage of the bill. It is a meticulous professional ritual.

You can linger – there's no pressure for you to leave your ringside seat in a café. The passing parade is fascinating: lottery ticket sellers, six men carrying a *marimba* like pall-bearers, a woman with kilos of shrimp in a plastic sack, the old men arguing over their domino game at the next table, the tiny children selling chewing-gum, and of course the musicians. Veracruz music can have a galloping Cuban beat, the *jarochas*, or a slightly melancholic, melodious resonance of *marimbas*. Mariachis are not lacking. Sometimes it's just one or two men with guitars who offer to play and sing for you. Indian boys from San Andrés de Tuxtla come by with bundles of handmade cigars for sale. Cheeky starlings with angry yellow eyes and a piercing whistle, like traffic cops, hop around for crumbs. By night the square and its fountain are

Children in Mexico are often the centre of attention.

lit up and the birds sing along with the music. It's as if Carnival had never stopped.

THE COAST

Gulf Coast beaches aren't all that fantastic. The best at Veracruz is **Mocambo**, a resort with hotel gardens, pools and restaurants on a very broad flat beach. The water is shallow a long way out. Farther on are **Boca del Río** and **Mandinga**, villages abounding in seafood restaurants and bars where *La Bamba* and similar *jarocha* songs are accompanied by the Veracruz 'harp' and guitars. 'Authentic' and 'seedy' are adjectives equally appropriate to these popular weekend retreats.

The spot where Cortés landed on 22 April 1519, is unmarked but presumed to be facing the little island of San Juan de Ulúa. The day was Good Friday and he later optimistically named his base **La Villa Rica de la Vera Cruz**, the 'Rich Town of the True Cross'. That base was moved several times to the present city limits. The first town, a few miles north, is now a village of cobbled streets, **La Antigua**, where the only monument is a bust of the national hero, Benito Juárez. About 40km (25 miles) north, off Route 180, are the ruins of **Zempoala**, the **Totonac** city where Cortés recruited allies that were to be crucial to his battles with the Aztecs. There are five partly reconstructed pyramid-temples and bits and pieces of Totonac buildings throughout the modern town.

OLMEC COUNTRY

The coastal hinterland between Veracruz and Villahermosa is the cradle of Mexican civilization, the home of the **Olmecs** from 1200 to around 400 BC. Little has survived of the cities they built of wood and mud brick in riverine areas that are now swampy and almost inaccessible. But the Olmecs left amazing works of art and influenced the cultures that followed.

To see a superb collection of these treasures, it is worth making the 96km (60-mile) trip to the state capital, **Xalapa** (*ha-LA-pa*, often spelt Jalapa). The road, which eventually reaches Puebla, winds up into cool highlands where you'll get a good view of the perpetual snows and perfect cone of the **Pico de**

Colourful market day in Chamula, Chiapas.

191

Orizaba, at 5,700m (18,551ft) the highest mountain in Mexico. Azaleas and camelias bloom in January in this cool mountain city of attractive, lush gardens. The light drizzle of the *chipi-chipi* rains keeps it refreshingly green.

The beautiful modern **Museo de Arqueología**, a work of art in itself, is one of the most important in Mexico. It has six of the huge Olmec basalt 'helmeted' heads. Some weighed 18 tonnes and were transported to the Olmec cities at San Lorenzo, Tres Zapotes and La Venta, probably by raft, as far as 128km (80 miles) from the nearest quarry.

Just as remarkable, the finely chiselled portraits were cut in this hard stone without metal tools. Yet after such effort, the heads were deliberately disfigured by the Olmecs and buried in the pits where they were first found in the 1930s. Why? Another of Mexico's mysteries.

The Olmecs worshipped a Jaguar God. Many figures in the museum are of a fanged half-human, half-animal 'were-jaguar'. There are also many of the curious laughing boys with flat triangular faces, four-wheeled animal toys in clay, figures with the artificially deformed heads copied by the Maya, superb portraits in terracotta, some painted and with holes in the head for inserting hair or feathers, and a model of a ball game that shows that this ritual, too, originated with the Olmecs. A particularly moving sculpture is of a priest holding in his lap the limp body of a sacrificed child. Surely this is one of the greatest museums of its kind. It is open from 10 a.m. to 5 p.m., closed Mondays.

The Xalapa museum contains a number of works from the Totonac city **El Tajín**. The remarkable feature of this important ruin is the **Temple of the Niches**, a six-layered pyramid, pierced by closely set window-like niches. These even open into the broad stair leading to the remains of a temple on the summit. The architecture of all the buildings at this large site is unlike anything else in Mexico. Some of the Totonac pottery boasts scroll designs and tripod feet that are very much like Chinese vessels.

El Tajín is a few miles from **Papantla**, the vanilla-growing home town of the *voladores*, the men who go spinning around at the end of long ropes hanging from a tall pole. Since they perform all over the country, one need not make the day-long round trip from Veracruz to see them on their native ground. But it is too bad that El Tajín is so far off the beaten track, for it is well worth a visit. North of this region is the oil-producing and shipping area around Tampico and Poza Rica, and then the long road to the Texas border at Matamoros-Brownsville.

El Tajín, in Veracruz, with the archaeological site in the background.

WHAT TO DO

SPORTS

Determined to provide everything a vacationer's heart could desire, resorts have laid on sports facilities to satisfy both players and spectators. **Tennis** courts are so plentiful, you rarely have to wait to play: Puerto Vallarta, to take just one example, has over 60. If you don't want to lug rackets around, rent them on the spot.

Fishing is one of the great sporting activities in Mexico.

The same goes for **golf**. Acapulco has three courses and they're in beautiful surroundings; the 19th hole at Cancún's Pok-ta-Pok could be a plunge into the lagoon. The five Mexico City courses are at private clubs, but a letter from your own club or hotel may get you a guest card. Cuernavaca's two courses are at a lower altitude, which makes life a bit easier on new arrivals. Golf is a major topic of conversation among the Las Hadas and Santiago crowd at Manzanillo. Some sportsmen come to Mexico just to keep up their golf and tennis during the winter months.

Water sports are tops. Scuba diving and snorkelling on the

Caribbean reefs is world class. So is **big game fishing** off Baja California and in the Sea of Cortés. Marinas at all coastal ports service yachts, and there's sailing on Lake Chapala, too. Hotels provide **waterskis**, **windsurfing** boards, **parasailing**, and noisy little **wave-runner runabouts**. Puerto Escondido has one of the best **surfing** beaches in the world, and there's good surfing at Huatulco and near Acapulco, as well. If **cliff-diving** is a sport and not a form of insanity, Acapulco has to have the champs.

Winter **hunting** of duck, geese, and doves on the Northern Mexico migratory flyway is terrific, but bringing in your guns can be com-plicated. Some camps rent guns and provide shells and licences. For up-to-date information on regulations, check with the Mexican Embassy or write to the Dirección de Flora y Fauna Silvestre, 20 Río Elba, Colonia Cuauhtémoc, Mexico, D.F, 06500. You can get a licence to hunt deer and puma, too. Jaguar and ocelot are protected.

Hiking and **backpacking** in the Copper Canyon area take you into real wilderness. You can **raft** or **kayak** down the gorge of the

Cozumel's clear waters are ideal for scuba diving.

Typical Mexican sweet specialities.

Usumacinta River. **Bike touring** in Baja, with an accompanying van to carry your luggage, is becoming popular. Baja seems made for rugged **off-the-road driving** with dune buggies and stock cars. After all, most of Baja is off the road! The **Baja Mil Millas** race kicks off at Tijuana and finishes at San Lucas del Cabo. It is a biennial November classic, conducted in a thrilling, if dusty, atmosphere. If you haven't had enough of cars in Mexico City traffic, you can always go to the **races** at the Autódromo de México, off the Viaducto Miguel Alemán.

Mexico has twice hosted the World Cup of **football** (soccer), and the 110,000-seat Azteca Stadium in the capital fills up for the big

on cable TV and shown in hotels with commentary in a feverish Spanish.

Then there's **horseracing** every day (except Monday and during Christmas and Easter weeks) at the beautiful Hipódromo de las Américas beyond Chapultepec Park in Mexico City (free admission if you show your Tourist Card at the entrance) and at Agua Caliente in Tijuana. Betting is also part of the excitement at the courts called *frontón* where the lightning-fast Basque version of handball, *jai-alai*, is played in the capital, Acapulco, and other major cities – players whip the ball with wicker scoops strapped to their hands.

Horseback riding is especially pleasant in the woods and fields around some of the hot spring resorts near Mexico City. Horses can also be rented in Chapultepec and Ajusco Parks in the city. Riding on the beach is fun in Mazatlán, Manzanillo and many other resorts. **Donkey polo**, played on the beach using brooms and a big ball, is a lark in Puerto Vallarta.

Charreadas, an intensely Mexican, super-macho kind of **rodeo** organized by horsemen's clubs, are held almost every Sunday noon at several rings in Mexico City, in Guadalajara and on occasion in other cities of the north. Finally, the season for the **Corrida de Toros**, or **bullfighting** in Mexico City, is from May to November in the world's largest ring, the 50,000-seat Plaza

matches. It hosted the Olympics in 1968. The Olympic stadium and other arenas built then are used now for regular matches of **boxing**, **wrestling** and **basketball**. Mexicans are *beisbol* fans, too, with league games in winter around the country. Don't be surprised to see a crowd cheering sandlot **baseball** under the lights on the beach at Veracruz. Major **American football** games, such as the Superbowl, are broadcast

197

The charreadas is Mexico's national sport.

México, off Insurgentes Sur. The programme starts punctually at 4 p.m. on Sunday. Tickets to *charreadas* and bullfights are often part of a tour, or can be bought through a travel agency. There are bullfights in Acapulco, Tijuana and most major cities during the season. It's the off-season in Spain, when many top *toreros* come to perform in Mexico.

SHOPPING

Sometimes a cliché is so apt it can't be avoided: let it be said once again that, yes, Mexico is a **paradise** for shoppers! The best advice from experienced market *aficionados* is 'Buy at least two of everything you like. If you don't, you'll wish you had later on.' Much of what we call handicrafts, *artesanías* in Spanish, are things Mexicans have been making for their own use for centuries. Some of it is pure Indian, with tribal variations, and some of it is an adaptation from the Spanish.

A tempting treat: chile rellenos.

Consider the wealth of articles recognizable anywhere as Mexican: fine, hand-loomed woolen *sarapes* (a kind of poncho); cotton or wool shawls of many colours, called *rebozos*; rugs in Indian designs; *huipiles*, the square-cut embroidered blouses worn in Yucatán; and *guayaberas*, fancy shirts men wear in the hot areas of the country. Pottery of all kinds, glazed, painted in designs unique to each locality, or just baked red clay, hand-blown glassware, naive paintings on bark or stitched in yarn, wildy exuberant Adam and Eve 'Tree of Life' candelabra. Or, grotesque masks used in Indian ceremonies, lacquerware, hundreds of straw products from baskets to Panama hats, wood-carved boxes, bedsteads, bannisters and what have you, not to mention leather goods such as *huarache* sandals, belts, jackets, wallets, handbags and hats. The tooled-leather saddles and boots are Mexican works of art. Where to stop the list? Silver jewellery, picture frames and ornaments can be a bargain, (but look for the '925' hallmark for sterling, or pay less). There are beautifully crafted vessels of copper, mirrors, lanterns and chandeliers of ornamental tin. Mexican opals, turquoise, lapis lazuli, onyx and other semi-precious stones and minerals are downright cheap. For the collector, genuine colonial antiques can be found as well as excellent copies. Toys and Christmas tree ornaments in painted tin are entrancing. Look

for scenes made of tiny figures inside nutshells and miniature doll furniture. You can get all your Christmas presents for years to come here, and highly original stocking-stuffers. Indian dolls and papier-mâché figures are unmistakeably Mexican. Gourds are carved, painted, lacquered and made into maracas, to shake, rattle and roll. An age-old tradition centres around *piñatas*, the candy-filled papier-mâché balloons in fanciful shapes, which are hung from the ceiling at Christmas and birthday parties to be broken by blindfolded, bat-wielding children.

Wherever you go in Mexico there will be a market, and in every market you are bound to find local handicrafts. The government's National Handicrafts Foundation (FONART)

Dolls made by the Chamula Indians, displayed at San Cristóbal de las Casas, make for colourful presents.

has shops at several locations in Mexico City and in major tourist centres. The municipal and state governments also operate *Mercados* and *Centros de Artesanías* and fixed-price shops found in museums. If you want to take your shopping seriously, it's useful to check the prices, quality and variety of goods in these places to compare for bargaining in the public markets and craft shops.

In the capital and holiday centres such as Acapulco, Cancún, Puerta Vallarta, Tijuana, etc., crafts from every part of the country are sold in the markets. This is good to know when you're grinding your teeth over a missed opportunity in Pátzcuaro or Oaxaca. But it's more fun and you'll enjoy your finds later on if you've bought them from the source, even seen them being made by village weavers and potters. You'll find more variety at the source, too, though prices won't be greatly lower.

Increased demand resulting from mass tourism has definitely lowered standards. You'll notice big differences in the hems, the stitching, the dyes, the finish of goods. Shop around and don't hesitate to point out what competing shops and stalls are offering. You may find, too, that established handicraft shops, while costing more, offer better quality than the big *artesanía* markets.

A papier-mâché sculpture, fit for any carnival float.

Here are some typical crafts and where to find them. Market days are marked in parenthesis, where appropriate:

• Acapulco: sportswear, all-Mexico shopping
• Acatlan (Puebla): 'Tree of Life' candlesticks, ceramics (Sun.)
• Chiapas de Corzo (Chiapas): lacquered gourds, masks
• Cuernavaca: bark paintings, baskets, silver, herbs (Sun.)
• Coyotepec (Oaxaca): black pottery
• Copper Canyon: Tarahumara baskets, hats, violins
• Guadalajara: glassware, silver, *charro* hats, pottery
• Guanajuato: silver, gold, minerals, skeleton candy and toys
• Jocotepec (Lake Chapala): white embroidered *sarapes* (Sun.)
• Mérida: *huipiles* and *guayaberas*, Panama hats, *huaraches*, gold
• Metepec (Puebla): 'Tree of Life' candlesticks (Mon.)
• Morelia: green pottery, woodwork, straw figures (Sun.)
• Mitla (Oaxaca): *rebozos*, *sarapes* (Thurs.)
• Oaxaca: baskets, pottery, wrought iron, *rebozos*, *sarapes* (Sat.)
• Ocotlán (Oaxaca): baskets, *sarapes*, rugs, leather (Fri.)
• Paracho (Mich.): guitars, violins
• Pátzcuaro: ceramics, lacquer, embroidery, rugs, baskets (Fri.)
• Puebla: ceramics, onyx, embroidery, tiles, saddles (Sun.)
• Puerto Vallarta: *huaraches*, textiles, jewellery, resort-wear

• Querétaro: amethysts, opals
• San Juan del Río: opals, *rebozos*
• San Miguel de Allende: tinware, ceramics, silver, mirrors, rugs
• San Cristóbal: leather, bags, weaving, embroidery
• Santa Clara del Cobre (Pátzcuaro): copperware
• Taxco: silver and gold jewellery
• Teotitlán del Valle (Oaxaca): *sarapes*, wool rugs
• Tlacolula (Oaxaca): pottery, embroidery, rugs (Sun.)
• Tlaquepaque (Guadalajara): pottery, furniture, glassware
• Uruapan: lacquer boxes and trays

ENTERTAINMENT

Generally speaking, people don't rave about Mexico's nightlife, but in the capital and larger cities as well as in the tourist centres you'll have a fair pick: from folkloric dance to modern theatre productions or cinema, jazz concerts, disco or simple mariachi music.

Mexico City's **Ballet Folklórico de México** is an institution, a show that everyone wants to see at least once. The setting, the Palacio de Bellas Artes and its Tiffany glass curtain of sunrise over the volcanoes and Valley of Mexico, is alone worth the price of admission. The programme recreates pre-Hispanic dances as well as Mexico's wonderfully varied regional music and fiestas, with gorgeous costumes. Performances are on Wednesdays and Sundays at 9p.m., with an

additional show at 7.30 p.m. on Sundays. Tickets are sold at the box office from 11 a.m. to 3 p.m. and 5 to 7 p.m. Monday through Saturday and from 8.30 a.m. to 1 p.m. and 4 to 9 p.m. on Sunday. An easy way to go is through a travel agency – it will provide good seats and pick you up at your hotel.

The Ballet Folklórico de México, in Mexico City, puts on a superb show and maintains an excellent reputation.

Tickets for the ballet and for sports, movies, bullfights and concerts can be bought at least 24 hours

203

in advance through **Bolestrónico**, a computerized service with outlets at the Insurgentes metro station in the Zona Rosa, the Bellas Artes lobby and other locations that your hotel should know about.

Touring companies of the Ballet Folklórico perform fairly regularly in Acapulco, Cancún and other cities. The provinces have quite good ballets of their own, too – Mérida's is one of the best. If you're in Oaxaca in late July-early August, get tickets to the *Guelaguetza*, held on two Mondays in the amphitheatre on the Cerro del Fortín overlooking the city. Dances of the state's seven regions are performed in native costumes, including the huge feather headdress of the *Danza de las Plumas*. Traditional entertainment accompanies all major holidays and the innumerable local fiestas. And every resort hotel worth the salt on its margarita glasses has a 'Fiesta Mexicana' night at least once a week.

Beautiful turn-of-the-century **theatres** have been restored in the Silver Cities and Oaxaca. Concerts, opera, musical comedy and stage plays are performed regularly in these gilt and velvet halls. Important cultural **festivals**, such as the October Cervantes Festival in Guanajuato, attract artists from around the world. And the cultural institutions of San Miguel de Allende, Guadalajara, Cuernavaca, Puebla and Morelia frequently schedule concerts and plays that can be enjoyed even without a knowledge of Spanish. Check the English-language *News* and local tourist information offices for details.

Acapulco is famous for its nightlife. Big bands, Latin beat orchestras, jazz groups, chorus lines of female impersonators, an active red-light district – it's all there. The top hotels advertise dinner with dancing and Las Vegas-style floorshows featuring international entertainers. Cancún and Ixtapa are quieter, but there are enough shows and discos to satisfy the most hyperactive holidaymakers.

For informal entertainment, go to the zócalo in any city or town around 8 p.m. and you'll probably find a **band** or a **marimba orchestra** up in the bird-cage bandstand going all out for an appreciative crowd. Often there will be dancing. In Mérida the evening show moves to a different plaza every night. In Veracruz, the music goes on from mid-morning until late at night. The Plaza Garibaldi in Mexico City and Plaza de los Mariachis in Guadalajara never sleep.

The Mexican **cinema** industry is thriving. Movies are a popular form of entertainment, with foreign films dubbed in Spanish. The *News* will advertise the films shown in English.

The ritual of the Pole Volador in the Sierra de Puebla.

ENTERTAINMENT

Fiestas

Somewhere in Mexico, you can be sure that a fiesta is underway right now. This has to be true, if only because every occupation and day of the year has a patron saint, because everybody has a birthday to share with neighbours and friends, because the seasons and the stars have always demanded recognition of their changes.

As inheritors of one of the first and most precise calendars, who should know this better than the

Mexicans? Where but in Oaxaca is there a 'Night of the Radishes'? (The zócalo is surrounded by stalls of long red radishes carved into figures, competing for a prize on 23 December.) Where but in Mexico do families stage an all-night vigil by the grave of a beloved departed, whilst picnicking and eating skull-shaped candies?

There are 13 official national holidays and 352 unofficial ones. Add one more for Leap Year. Don't count on the unofficial ones being celebrated on the same day each year. If a jolly fiesta falls in midweek, some towns might decide to have the party on the weekend. Because of the strong secular character of the Reform and Revolution, none of the national holidays has religious significance except Christmas and Easter. Yet all the most important fiestas follow the Roman Catholic calendar.

At the same time, the true spirit underlying a celebration that begins with Mass at the church, may come out into the plaza with masked dancers and offerings carried over from ancient Indian rites. Only anthropologists really care about such matters – for the participants a fiesta is a fiesta: a time for dressing up, marching in parades, decorating the zócalo with strings of lights or festoons of cutout paper, setting off fireworks and boosting the decibels, eating, drinking, dancing and being together with the whole family. In most cases, visitors can join the fray, but in some Indian villages, photography of rites is not allowed and onlookers should watch discreetly.

A festival in Tehuantepec (Oaxaca).

WINING AND DINING

Mexican cuisine rates as one of the world's most varied and unusual. Don't confuse it with the chile-powder-dosed 'Mexican Platters' of the US border states. The best Mexican cooking combines fresh ingredients not usually available outside the country and lots of loving labour of grinding, chopping and blending. It also blends ancient Indian traditions with European materials and recipes, for until the Spanish colonials came, the only meat available in Mexico was game, turkey and dog. (Not to mention the flesh of human sacrifices, of course.)

The restaurants of Mexico City, as in any great capital, offer specialities from around the world. But what's surprising is the number of different *Mexican* cuisines represented. What's sauce for the goose in Sinaloa doesn't garnish the gander in Quintana Roo. The provincial cities all have their own special dishes and recipes, their favourite ingredients, and even international resort hotels serve some authentic Mexican dishes. After all, Mexicans are among their most regular clients.

One might ask where 'international' food would be without the contributions originating in Mexico. Italy, for example, without tomato sauce? Switzerland without chocolate? France without vanilla? The US without peanuts? And that's not counting avocados, various kinds of squash, peppers and beans and above

'Happy Hour' in Acapulco.

all, maize. One might add the after-dinner cigar, which comes from the Mayan word *xigar*, meaning 'to suck'.

A Mexican's **breakfast** is often an early *café con leche* (coffee and milk) or hot chocolate, followed around 10.30 with *botanas*, substantial snacks wrapped in a tortilla hot from the *comal*, the curved cooking tin placed over charcoal. Or perhaps sweet *pan dulce* cakes, taken in a café or at a sidewalk stand. Hotels spread lavish buffets to satisfy both Mexican and foreign tastes. After the first day you'll be taking refried beans along with your scrambled eggs, or maybe *huevos rancheros* on

Tortillas sprinkled with mushrooms and herbs will be made into tacos.

a tortilla with a tomato and red chile sauce, or *chilaquiles* – tortilla chips with crumbled sausage or cheese and onions in a creamy sauce.

The traditional main Mexican meal, a solid **lunch**, beginning around 2 p.m. and lasting for a good couple of hours, is giving way in the big cities to lighter and faster meals. Traffic jams and tighter office schedules are to blame. The siesta is a casualty of the same forces. The *comida corrida*, the one-price complete menu of the day, is served only at lunch and is often the best buy. **Dinner** is when foreigners want to live it up, so restaurants are geared to laying on the big meal again in the evening – usually after 8 p.m.

Mexico City has some sensationally beautiful restaurants installed in the salons and gardens of old ha-

ciendas, at the top of skyscrapers, in parks overlooking lakes, and in cabarets often accompanied by violins or entire music-and-dance troupes. You'll find them tucked away in turn-of-the-century dining rooms or in tile-walled popular eateries in the old centre. In the coastal resorts you'll eat outdoors, on terraces above the sea. In the colonial cities, cafés under the arcades of the zócalo will tempt you. And if you get homesick for your own native fare, whether hamburgers or hassenpfef-

The sign 'Dulceria' on the door indicates this shop's speciality: all things sweet.

fer, you'll find there's an expatriate restaurant catering to your whim, just around the corner.

Besides the scores of chiles used in Mexican cookery, a number of **herbs** are essential, such as *cilantro* (fresh coriander), *epazote*, ground nuts and pumpkin seeds. Limes and bitter orange are important, too. A fruit-juice stand may serve drinks made from mamey, *guayaba*, *zapote*, papaya, *chirimoya* and *guanábana*, as well as the more familiar and non-native coconut, banana and orange.

Soups are often a meal in themselves, called *pucheros*. In Yucatán, the *sopa de lima* is much more than a simple lime soup. It is loaded with chicken and tortilla chips. In Jalisco, the *pozole* is virtually a stew, containing maize hominy, pork and vegetables. The capital favours *sopa Tlalpeño*, a chicken broth with green beans, carrots, avocado and chickpeas. The morning after New

Year's Eve, nothing will do but *sopa de menudo*, of tripe and hominy with hot chile and limes on the side. *Sopa seca* is generally a pasta or a rice dish.

Antojitos are supposed to be **appetizers**, but they will fill even the hungriest pyramid-climber. They

range from *cilantro*-flavoured guacamole, the avocado purée scooped up with tortilla chips, to the soda-glass filled with conch, shrimp, octopus and oysters in a red-hot cocktail sauce aptly called *vuelve a la vida*, or 'return to life'. Fried pork bits (*carnitas*) are wrapped in a tortilla and generously doused with chile sauce. Anything else wrapped in a tortilla is usually called a *taco*, the most ubiquitous Mexican snack.

Among the **fish** dishes, red snapper in a garlicky tomato sauce with mild chiles, capers and olives is the most famous: *huachinango a la veracruzana*. *Pompano* is a treat, when you can get it, and so is a good pickled fish or seafood *ceviche*. Shrimp (*camarones*) and lobster (*langosta*) are almost everyday fare in the beach resorts.

No one should fail to try Puebla's *mole poblano* sauce of bitter chocolate and 23 'secret' ingredients (several different chiles, nuts, cloves, cinnamon, coriander, sesame seeds, garlic and anise are among them) served on turkey (*guajolote*). Oaxaca has tasty black, red and green moles, too. And the shredded, pit-roasted suckling pig of Yucatán, *cochinita pibil* in a bitter orange sauce, is another must for the gourmet.

Sunday at Xochimilco: an infectious party atmosphere is guaranteed to get under your skin.

The absolute emperor of stuffed peppers is *chiles en nogada*. Large *poblano* peppers are filled with minced pork seasoned with almonds, garlic and spices, fried, and covered with a delicate sauce of fresh ground walnuts in sour cream, then topped with fresh, ruby-red pomegranate seeds. All this is definitely a far cry from *chile con carne*.

Desserts in hotels tend toward the usual flan egg custards, sometimes coated with coconut, or rice pudding and ice creams, but in the countryside you may be offered *dulce de camote*, a sweet yam pudding, or *chongos*, curds in syrup. In Oaxaca, especially at Christmas, everyone eats flaky, deep-fried *buñuelos* (crepes in syrup), served during the holidays in bowls that you smash after eating for good luck. Probably the best way to end a meal is with fruit, so varied, plentiful and fresh in Mexico. Go to the markets. Have you ever seen redder watermelons, juicier strawberries, such pineapples bursting with sweetness, and so many exotic species?

Beer is *the* drink to accompany Mexican food. The many brands satisfy every taste, from the sweetish dark brews to light dry lagers. Familiar soft drinks are bottled under licence in Mexico and each region seems to have its local favourite

On offer at this market stall: unrefined sugar.

mineral water, plain (*sin gas*) or sparkling (*con gas*). Mexican-grown **coffee** varies according to local tastes, too. The strong expresso of Veracruz is one of the best. *Café de olla*, cooked in an earthenware pot, is spiced with cinnamon, cloves and raw brown sugar. Tea drinkers won't appreciate the practice of bringing a tea bag with a fast-cooling pot of water. Herbal teas, such as *manzanilla*, are a better bet and soothing to the tummy, too.

Wine is getting better and better, thanks to serious efforts to improve vintages by new investors, including some well-known Spanish houses with vineyards in Baja California and northern states. Imported wines and hard spirits are very expensive. National distilleries make good rum and passable gin and vodka. **Tequila**, of course, is the national tipple. It is made from the sap of a special maguey, the agave plant. **Mezcal**, from Oaxaca, comes from another maguey, and is available in a yellowed *añejo* (aged) version and the clear *pechuga*. **Pulque** is the juice of yet another maguey, but it is fermented, not distilled, and has a lower alcohol content. This is a drink of countrymen, for it has to be consumed when quite fresh. It is thick and cloudy with a tang, like buttermilk, and may be *curado*, flavoured with strawberries, pineapple or other fruits. So enjoy yourself, and as Mexicans say when seeing others eat, '*Buen provecho!*', May it do you good!

BERLITZ-INFO

CONTENTS

BLUEPRINT FOR A PERFECT TRIP

A ACCOMMODATION (*alojamiento*). (See also CAMPING)

Hotel prices are government regulated according to categories that range from lavish to minimal, but star ratings don't tell the whole story. A charming hotel in an old mansion may charge low rates simply because it doesn't have TV or a pool, while run-of-the-mill hostelries that feature such amenities may cost twice as much. Also, depending on the various package deals available and seasonal discounts, the same lodging may go for very different prices. A travel agent with Mexican experience can be a great help in giving advice tailored to your needs.

Along with the local choices, virtually all of the major international hotel chains are represented in Mexico. Be aware that rates at the beaches and other resorts are higher (and harder to negotiate) from mid-December until Easter. You'll need advance bookings for this popular period. Travellers arriving without reservations will find hotel information desks, phones, and sometimes complimentary transport in the major airports. For the budget-conscious visitor, the most economical accommodation can be found at simple **guest houses** (*casa de huéspedes*). And in general, the cheapest hotels will always be found in the city centre near the bus terminals or around the zócalo.

All beach resorts now feature 'time-sharing' **apartments**. Many are connected to hotels, so you can make inquiries through a travel agent or hotel upon arrival. **Furnished apartments** (*amueblados* or *suites*) are another option. If you plan to spend a few weeks in Mexico at one place, it is easy to rent such self-catering apartments that often include hotel services in the price. Try looking in the ads of the morning paper or ask a travel agent.

Mexico has a network of **youth hostels** (*albergue de juventud*), but it isn't very extensive. For information, write to:

Asociación Mexicana de Albergues de la Juventud
Glorieta Metro Insurgentes, Local C-11, Col. Juárez, Mexico City,
CP06600, tel. (5) 525-2548/525-2974/525-2916/525-2699

I'd like a single/double room	**Quisiera una habitación sencilla/doble**
with bath/shower.	**con baño/regadera.**
What's the rate per night?	**¿Cuál es el precio por noche?**
Where is there a cheap hotel?	**¿Dónde hay un hotel económico?**

AIRPORT

Benito Juárez International Airport in Mexico City is actually inside the city limits. It handles about 35,000 passengers and a 'floating population' of some 100,000 persons a day. There are seven national and 26 international airlines represented, and it may appear a great buzzing confusion at first, but just take it slow and easy. Follow the signs to your luggage pickup point (*entrega de equipajes*), which will be Area E or D for international flights and B for most national arrivals. Look for a booth marked 'Taxis' where you can buy a ticket for a fixed-price cab to your hotel. (There are booths inside the luggage area and also a ticket window outside Area A at the far left of the hall when you exit with your bags.) You may have a porter take your bags as they come off the moving belt, but he can't leave the luggage area. You will have to take a second porter beyond that point. Tip about the equivalent of US 50 cents per bag. Clearance through customs is fairly quick.

In the long hall outside the luggage areas, you will find banks and cambios (private money changers, who give almost the same rate as a bank), where you can buy and sell your dollars and pesos. There are souvenir shops, bookstores and newstands, places to eat and drink, hotel and travel information services, a post office (near Area A), one hotel linked to the terminal by a walkway and another nearby that is served by free shuttle buses, left-luggage lockers (*depósito de equipajes*) and many other useful services. Pay no attention to people calling 'Taxi!' or to anyone offering guide services. If you need help, go to one of the information booths. (Telephones located at intervals along the mall are free for calls within the city. There are special phones for long distance, so marked.) You may have to stand in line at busy hours to get your airport cab at the end of Area A. When you get to the head of the line, tell the dispatcher your destination, which he will relay to the cab driver. Give your pre-paid ticket to the driver, then sit back and relax.

This information applies more or less to all cities of Mexico, where yellow and white mini-vans marked *transportación terrestre* are pre-paid inside the airport or just outside on the sidewalk. If you prefer to take your own cab and not wait while the shared van drops off other customers, ask the price to your destination before entering the cab to avoid any unpleasant surprises. Private cab rates will run ten to fifteen dollars, compared to five dollars or less for the in-bound airport service. Airport taxis aren't allowed to pick up passengers in town. There is an airport departure tax of about $10 per person for international flights.

Guadalajara's international airport has daily flights to points in the US and Canada and Alaska, as well as connections to the coast and throughout Mexico.

| Porter! | **Maletero!** |
| Where's the bus for ...? | **¿Dónde está el camión para ...?** |

B BARGAINING

Street, market and beach vendors and modest handicraft stands are all prepared to bargain. Hotel gift shops, government handicraft outlets, department stores and fine boutiques all have fixed prices. A cagey shopper will see what the fixed-price shops are charging and eavesdrop on the bargaining of other shoppers – if none of this is possible, you should start out offering about 20 per cent less than you are willing to pay. However, you shouldn't enter into the haggling game unless really ready to buy, and not propose a price that is insultingly below what the seller is asking. You can always break off a deadlock in a pleasant way, saying '*gracias*', and indicating that you want to look around. When you come back, you'll probably be able to knock at least 20 per cent off the asking price without shedding blood. And if haggling upsets you, simply ask if there is a discount (*¿Me hace una rebaja?*). Rest assured that whatever you finally pay, the seller is making a profit and you probably have your bargain.

C CAMPING

There is camping throughout the country, including two camping sites in Mexico City itself plus several others in the surrounding area, but you'll find organized campgrounds (KAO) only in the north. Certain hotels may have places for camping. Except in Baja, sleeping or camping on the beach is not advisable because of attacks and robbery. For more information write for the brochure 'Camping in Mexico':

Tourism Office, Mariano Escobedo 726, Mexico City, CP11590, tel. (5) 211-0099

May we camp here?	¿Podemos acampar aquí?
We have a tent/trailer.	Tenemos una tienda de campaña/una caravana.

CAR HIRE (*automoviles de alquiler*). (See also DRIVING IN MEXICO) All well known international companies and many reliable national ones rent to persons 25 years of age with a valid driver's licence. They will accept credit cards. Insurance costs about $25 per day. Rates will vary, of course, but you can expect to pay approximately $35 to $60 per day with unlimited mileage. Shop around for the best deal.

I'd like to rent a car for today/tomorrow.	Quisiera rentar un coche para hoy/mañana.
for one day/one week	por un día/una semana

CLOTHING

The lightest and most informal summer clothing is fine for all the beach resorts year round, but you should bring a light sweater and windbreaker for the occasional cool mornings and evenings; also keep in mind that at high altitudes and in the desert, winter can be quite cold. A raincoat or umbrella will come in handy from May to October. Ties and jackets for men are virtually unknown at beach resorts but are commonly worn in the better restaurants of the big cities, particularly in the evening. Don't wear miniskirts or shorts (the latter goes for men as well) anywhere in Mexico apart from the big tourist resorts. As a general rule, in the more remote villages both men and women should take care to dress conservatively.

Sandals as well as a comfortable pair of walking shoes (for scrambling over ruins and pyramids) are a must.

COMMUNICATIONS

Post offices (*correos*) Hotel desks will promise to stamp and mail letters for you, but to be safe, stock up on stamps at a post office. In Mexico City, the Central Post Office is on Calle Tacuba next to the Palacio de Bellas Artes. There is also one at the airport.

Opening hours are usually from 9 a.m. to 7 p.m., often closing on Saturdays at 1.30 p.m. In the capital though, the post office is open from 7 a.m. to midnight, Monday through Friday, closing at 8 p.m. on Saturday and 4 p.m. on Sunday.

General Delivery (*poste restante*) If you don't know in advance where you'll be staying, you can have your mail addressed to the *Lista de Correos* in any town. They'll hold your mail for ten days before returning it. In Mexico City, this service is at Window 6 on the main floor of the Central Office. Take identification with you to collect mail.

Mailboxes (*buzón*) If you have a choice of slots, always put international mail in the one marked *Aereo* (air mail); *Terrestre* is for surface mail. In Mexico City, *D.F.* is for local mail. On postcards you can overlap several stamps to save space as long as the denomination is showing.

Telegrams Telegrams and cables must be sent from the telegraph office (*Oficina de Telégrafos*), which is often separate from the post. In Mexico City this is at Balderas 15, near the west end of the Alameda, and is open from 8 a.m. to midnight daily. The district post office on Calle Estrasburgo in the Zona Rosa has a **fax** service, as do many hotels around the country.

Telephone Public coin-operated telephones are liberally spread about Mexico City's streets and public buildings and most of them are free, even though instructions tell you to put in a 20-centavo or 1-peso coin. Free phone facilities were provided to help families in the aftermath of the earthquake. When inflation changed the value and size of coins, this couldn't be changed without overhauling the whole system.

Some new phones require coins and register the credit as you deposit them. Mexico has sold the national company, so this situation may not continue long. Generally speaking, any change will be for the better in a phone system that is admittedly inadequate. Be forewarned that long-distance calls, whether within Mexico or abroad, are horrendously expensive. Hotel operators will often ask whether you want to call collect (*por cobrar*) – in fact, this will save you money. You can also phone from operator-attended long distance offices in some airports and around town. Locations are listed in the front of telephone directories. Where these don't exist, there are private services, usually storefronts with a sign '*larga distancia*'. The owner will place your call and charge you a small fee. Long-distance calls can be made direct but only from private phones.

In Mexico City, dial **01** (information in Mexico), **06** (police/emergency), **07** (information in Spanish and English), **09** (international operator), and **02** (long-distance national operators, rarely speaking English).

The following is a list of some useful indexes (*ladas*). You'll need to dial the index + area code + number.

Within Mexico:

Station to station, direct dialling	**91**
Person to person, direct dialling	**92**

International:

Station to station, direct, US + Canada	**95**
Person to person, US + Canada	**96**
Person to person, rest of the world	**99**
(dial 98 + country code + area code + number)	

Can you get me this number?	**¿Puede comunicarme a este número?**
collect (reversed-charged) call	**por cobrar**
person-to-person (personal) call	**de persona a persona**
I want to send a telegram to ...	**Quisiera mandar un telegrama a ...**
Have you received any mail for...?	**¿Ha recibido correo para...?**
stamp/letter/postcard	**timbre/carta/tarjeta**
special delivery (express)	**urgente**
airmail	**correo aéreo**
registered	**registrado**

COMPLAINTS (*reclamación*)

If you have a complaint against a hotel, restaurant, taxi driver or tourist guide, and you can't work it out on the spot, go to the Tourism Office. There you'll find the Dirección General de Supervisión, which deals with such problems.

For grievances involving people or organizations not normally associated with the tourism industry, it's recommended that you go to the local police station. In Mexico City, the tourism office is located at:

Secretaría de Turismo, Av. Presidente Masaryk 172, Polanco, Mexico 11587, D.F. tel. (5) 250-0151/0123/0493.

CONVERSION CHARTS
Temperature

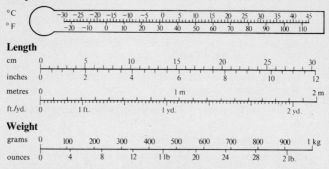

Length

Weight

COURTESIES AND SOCIAL CUSTOMS
Mexicans are by nature and upbringing dignified and courteous. Passengers leaving a bus may say '*gracias*' (thank you) to the driver and receive a '*para servirle*' (at your service) in reply. If you sneeze, someone will be sure to say *salud*, to which you reply *gracias*. Always address any stranger as Señor or Señorita (even older women, unless you know they are married). Liberally use *gracias*, *por favor* (please) and *muy amable* (very kind of you) to smooth any transaction. Shaking hands upon meeting and leaving is expected. Don't be surprised if the handshake is a double-action grip involving locking thumbs. Men friends often greet each other with a bear hug and back-slapping, called an *abrazo*; women will kiss each other on the cheek and may walk arm-in-arm down the street.

Mexicans are sensitive to criticism and regard most non-Latins as unrealistically demanding and inflexible. Before loudly complaining about some apparent inefficiency, pause and remember the annoyances you complain about in your own country. You'll probably discover that, on balance,

Mexico does not suffer by comparison and has many delightful compensations. Your best investment will be a smile. It is always repaid, and with dividends.

Be aware that a Mexican's desire to please and avoid the negative may lead to waiters not bringing the bill until requested, clerks not volunteering that tomorrow is a holiday and the office is closed, strangers giving directions to places they've never heard of, and people agreeing to things they'll never carry out and accepting invitations they won't honour. Students of these matters say that the ancient Indian belief that only the gods decide destiny survives today in an attitude of futility concerning definite plans. There may be something to this. The *mañana* stereotype, though, like the one of the Mexican snoozing under a big *sombrero*, bears little resemblance to the hard working artisans, farmers, factory and office workers who turn the wheels of modern Mexico. The *siesta* is a thing of the past in most big cities, though lunchtime closing hours are observed in the provinces.

If you have a business meeting, be aware that a Mexican will begin with small-talk about families or the weather; to plunge straight into business is considered bad form.

Women should keep in mind that the attitudes prevalent in this country tend to view foreign women, especially those travelling alone, as promiscuous and sexually available. The only way around eventual misunderstandings is to dress and behave conservatively, and not to respond in any way to various attentions and provocations. Women shouldn't have any trouble being served in hotels or regular bars and restaurants, but they are not admitted into local *cantinas* or *pulquerías*. In fact, in certain places even foreign men won't be allowed into the *pulquerías*.

CRIME

Pickpockets operate wherever there are crowds, such as the Basilica of Guadalupe, at flea markets, and in the Metro. Be alert. There is a brisk trade in US passports. Don't leave yours in the hotel room – use the hotel safe for valuables and use the chain lock on your hotel room. Always lock your car; don't leave valuables in sight. Don't leave luggage or packages unattended at the airport or outside the hotel.

In Mexico City, Plaza Garibaldi is one of the high crime rate areas. You'll want to avoid it after the early evening hours, when the tour buses depart.

I want to report a theft.	**Quiero denunciar un robo.**

CUSTOMS AND ENTRY REGULATIONS

Formalities at a border or airport are quick and simple. Instead of a visa, visitors must have a **tourist card**, obtainable upon proof of citizenship from airlines serving Mexico and at border points. This free card is valid for three months and is renewable for another three, though the renewal process is very time-consuming. It will be stamped on entry and must be kept with you for presentation on departure. Carry your card with you at all times – if you lose it, report this to the local tourist office at once to avoid delays on departure. US citizens may visit Mexico for 72 hours without a tourist card.

You may bring into Mexico 12 rolls of film and video cassettes, 500 cigarettes or 100 cigars or 250 grams of pipe tobacco, and three litres of spirits or wine.

The following chart shows what main duty-free items you may take into Mexico and, when returning home, to your own country:

	Cigarettes		Cigars		Tobacco	Spirits		Wine
Mexico	400	or	50	or	250g	3l	or	3l
Australia	250	or	200	or	250g	1.1l	or	1.1l
Canada	200	or	50	and	1kg	1.1l	or	1.1l
Eire	200	or	50	or	250g	1l	or	2l
N Zealand	200	or	50	or	250g	1.1l	and	4.5l
S Africa	400	and	50	and	250g	1l	and	2l
UK	200	or	50	or	250g	1l	and	2.
USA	200	and	100	and	*	1l	and	1l

* A reasonable quantity

Currency restrictions Non-residents may import or export any amount of freely convertible foreign currency into Mexico, provided it is declared upon arrival. There is also no limit to the amount of Mexican currency you may carry into or out of Mexico.

| I have nothing to declare. | **No tengo nada que declarar.** |

DRIVING IN MEXICO   D

Any valid driver's licence is accepted in Mexico. To rent a car, the driver must be at least 25 years of age. If you bring your own car, you must present proof of ownership at the border, where it will be registered with your tourist card. If anyone other than the owner of the car is planning to drive it while in Mexico, be sure to make arrangements at the customs. You may need to present proof of ownership when boarding car ferries. Take out full accident and liability Mexican insurance at the border: US insurance doesn't apply.

Most Mexican surfaced roads are two laners, very winding in the mountains and often without shoulders. While the main highways are in generally good condition, be careful rounding curves and topping rises: there may be cows or a poorly signalled hazard just out of sight. Try to avoid driving at night when visibility is bad. Rocks or branches on the road mean there's a vehicle broken down ahead. If you have car trouble, raise your hood and wait for the 'Green Angels' (*Angeles Verdes*). These green government repair trucks patrol the main routes from 8 a.m. to 9 p.m., make minor repairs and supply emergency petrol, charging only the cost of the materials. They are equipped with radios and can be called on Citizen Band frequencies. A passing car or truck can also alert the Green Angels on your behalf.

Have your car thoroughly checked before departure and bring along any spare parts, such as a fan belt and oil filter, which may be difficult to obtain. A container of water and a petrol-can are good insurance.

Pemex is the government monopoly petrol station. It sells super (*extra*) and regular (*nova*), and unleaded petrol in an increasing number of stations. Octane ratings are not the same as in the US though, and if your motor 'pings', you can try an additive to slow combustion. Discuss with your mechanic the advisability of disconnecting your catalytic converter if you are planning to do a lot of driving in Mexico. Fill up whenever your tank is half empty: it may be a long drive to the next station. Petrol station attendants should be tipped for filling the tank or for other services. Foreign credit cards are not accepted at filling stations.

Look out for signs in villages and near schools announcing *topes* or *vibradores*. These are humps placed across the road to slow traffic and are nasty to hit at high speed. The top speed limit is 100km/h (60mph). Get a good road map from your automobile club (they are not sold in petrol stations); it will also describe the common road signs. An 'E' (*estacionamiento*) in a circle with a line through it means 'No Parking'. When approaching a narrow bridge, the first car to flash its lights has right of way.

Visitors are strongly advised to avoid driving in Mexico City if they can. The *periférico* expressways circling the city intersect with *ejes*, arterial routes to the centre; buses using an express lane may seem to be coming at you in the wrong direction on these one-way arteries. Many downtown streets are narrow and/or one-way and the traffic is fiendish. Once you get near the centre, you can make your way to the Paseo de la Reforma, which runs from Chapultepec Park to the Alameda Park. Once there, enjoy yourself – put your car in a garage and get around town by taxi, bus and metro. The city centre is well supplied with parking meters and multi-storied car parks. Uniformed parking lot attendants operate in other busy zones; as you leave you should give the attendant a few pesos.

Fluid measures

imp. gals.	0			5		10

liters	0	5	10	20	30	40	50

U.S. gals.	0		5		10	

Distance

km	0	1	2	3	4	5	6	8	10	12	14	16
miles	0	½	1	1½	2	3	4	5	6	7	8	9	10

Most Mexican road signs are the standard international pictographs. But you may encounter these written signs:

Aduana	Customs
Alto	Stop
Autopista (de peaje)	(Toll) highway
Camino deteriorado	Bad road
Ceda el paso	Yield
Cruce peligroso	Dangerous crossing
Cuidado	Caution
Despacio	Slow

Desviación	Detour
Escuela	School
Peligro	Danger
Prohibido estacionarse	No parking
Prohibido rebasar	No passing
Puesto de socorro	First-aid station
Puente angosto	Narrow bridge
Salida de camiones	Truck exit
(International) driver's licence	**Licencia para manejar (internacional)**
Car registration papers	**registro del automóvil**
Are we on the right road for ...?	**¿Es ésta la carretera hacia ...?**
Fill the tank, top grade, please.	**Llénelo, por favor, con super.**
Check the oil/tires/battery.	**Revise el aceite/las llantas/la batería.**
I've had a breakdown.	**Mi carro se ha descompuesto.**
There's been an accident.	**Ha habido un accidente.**

DRUGS

For all the talk about 'Acapulco Gold', drugs are illegal and not tolerated in Mexico. Drug-dealers will often set up others for arrest by the police, and if you're caught it will be very difficult to avoid jail. And if picked up by Federal Police, you can be held indefinitely without trial.

ELECTRIC CURRENT   E

Mexico is on the US and Canadian system of 120 volts and 60 cycles and the plug with two flat pins. Appliances using other systems will require a transformer and adaptor plug best brought with you.

EMBASSIES AND CONSULATES (*embajada*)

In Mexico City
Canada
Schiller 529, Colonia Polanco, Mexico City, CP 11570, tel. (5) 254-3288
Great Britain
Río Lerma 71, Mexico City, CP 06050, tel. (5) 207-2089
USA
Av. Reforma 305, Mexico City, CP 06500, tel. (5) 211-0042 or 555-3333
Saturdays

Elsewhere
Canada
Hotel Fiesta Americana L-30, Guadalajara, Jalisco, CP 44100,
tel. (36) 253-434/158-665
Centro Commercial Plaza Mexico, Local 312, Av. Tulum 200, Cancún,
Quintana Roo, CP 77500, tel. (988) 43716/33393
Great Britain
Calle 58 x 53 No. 450, Mérida, Yucatán, tel. (99) 16799
USA
Progresso 175, Guadalajara, Jalisco, CP 44100, tel. (36) 252-988
Consular representative in Acapulco, Hotel Club de Sol, Costera Miguel
Aleman, Raíz Católicos, Acapulco, Guerrero, CP 39580, tel. (748) 57207
Parian del Puente, Local 12-A, Puerto Vallarta, Jalisco, CP 48300,
tel.(322) 20069
Victimas 25 de Junio No. 388, Veracruz, Veracruz, CP 91700, tel. (29) 315-821
Alcala 201, Oficina 206, Oaxaca, Oaxaca, CP 78000, tel. (951) 43054
Av. Nader 40, Oficina 31, Cancún, Quintana Roo, CP 77500, tel.
(988) 42411
Paseo Montejo 453, Mérida, Yucatán, CP 97000, tel. (99) 255-011

G GUIDES
All sorts of ingratiating types will offer to be helpful. If you want a guide,
get one who is accredited by the Secretariat of Tourism through your hotel or a travel agency. At major museums and archaeological sites, tours
by official guides speaking foreign languages are available and can increase
your enjoyment. It is customary to give tour guides a tip.

We'd like an English-speaking guide.	**Queremos un guía que hable inglés.**
I need an English interpreter.	**Necesito un intérprete de inglés.**

HEALTH

No vaccinations are required for entry, but your doctor may recommend updating your tetanus and polio immunization and suggest gamma globulin as a hepatitis deterrent. Mexico City and some other towns are over 1,335m (7,000ft) an altitude that will affect some visitors more than others. If you notice shortness of breath, slight headache and a tired feeling, take it easy on exercise, food and drink for the first day or two and the symptoms will disappear. Along with the altitude, the pollution will probably be a definite change from what you're used to. Breathing the air of this city in one average day is equivalent to smoking two packs of cigarettes. Don't even try to imagine what a bad day means.

The most notorious Mexican health hazard, variously known as the *turista* or 'Moctezuma's Revenge', is a relatively harmless combination of diarrhoea and stomach upset that travellers encounter worldwide. It almost always comes from the water. The best way to avoid this nuisance is never drink water from a tap or offered in a glass and never take ice. Drink only bottled water, soft drinks or beer and don't even brush your teeth in tap water; ask for bottled water. Many hotels provide jugs of purified water (*agua purificada*) or have purified water taps. The machine-made ice cubes in first-class establishments are usually safe, but usually doesn't mean always: you can ask for drinks *sin hielo* (without ice). It's hard to pass up the delicious fruits and juices in markets or the savoury snacks offered at street stands, but it's best to play it safe until you've been in the country a couple of weeks and have made peace with the unfamiliar local bacteria. If you do succumb, take plenty of liquids with a little salt and sugar, such as black tea or a herbal tea like manzanilla. Let your doctor prescribe any drugs to take along for this problem. Opinion is divided on the use of anti-diarrhoea pills and antibiotics. If you're caught short, Mexican pharmacies can sell most drugs without prescription (but not sleeping pills or tranquillizers) and are familiar with proven local remedies for *turista*. Outside of regular opening hours (i.e. evenings and holidays) certain pharmacies remain 'on duty'; the location of the nearest one on duty will be posted in the window of all pharmacies.

In an emergency, most hotels have a doctor on call who will speak English. There are English-speaking staff at:

American-British Hospital, Calle Sur 136, Colonia Américas, Mexico City, tel. (5) 272-850

México-Americano Hospital, Colomos 2110, Guadalajara, tel. (36) 410-089/414-458

HOURS

In the capital and major resorts, such as Acapulco and Cancún, shops and offices open at 9 a.m. and remain open until 6 p.m. or even later. Almost everywhere museums are open from 9 a.m. to 5 p.m., and banks from 9 a.m. to 3 p.m. Provincial offices and the small shops of big cities close from around 1.30 to 4 p.m. for *siesta*, then stay open until around 7 or 8 p.m. There is no set rule about this for the whole country, so try to find out in advance if you intend to shop or do business.

L LANGUAGE

Mexico is the largest Spanish-speaking country in the world and Spanish follows Chinese and English as the most widely spoken language of this planet. In addition, Mexican Indians speak 58 indigenous languages, with Spanish as their *lingua franca*. English is understood in hotels and tourist-oriented establishments throughout the country – even Indian market women may be able to quote prices in English. Official guides qualified in major European languages and Japanese may be engaged through travel agencies or located through the National Tourism Secretariat (SECTUR), Calle Mariano Escobedo 726, Mexico City, CP 11590, tel. (5) 211-0099. But any Spanish you possess or phrases you learn will be appreciated by Mexicans and will make asking directions, shopping and ordering food easier.

The Berlitz phrase book, LATIN-AMERICAN SPANISH FOR TRAVELLERS, covers most situations you are likely to encounter in your visit to Mexico; also useful is the Berlitz English-Spanish pocket dictionary, containing a special menu-reader supplement. (See also USEFUL EXPRESSIONS.)

LOST PROPERTY

Every state and major city of Mexico has a Tourist Department with a telephone number for tourist assistance. (See TOURIST INFORMATION.) If your hotel can't solve your problem, ask them to contact this number or the local Policía Judicial for you.

Lost children will normally be delivered to the neighbourhood police station, which is where you should go if you lose a child – or find one. You can also telephone 'Locatel' – in Mexico City (5) 658-11-11 – a computerized information service, which will research the whereabouts of lost children.

I've lost my wallet/purse/passport.	**He perdido mi cartera/bolsa/ pasaporte.**

MEETING PEOPLE

M

Mexicans are exceptionally friendly people, once you overcome their initial reserve. This can be accomplished swiftly by a smile and a question or remark in Spanish. If someone recognizes your accent and can speak your language, they will be delighted to demonstrate it.

Mexican women follow rigid codes of behaviour and may not respond if they misinterpret your interest. On the other hand, men who approach you, usually on the street and often asking 'Where are you from?', are most certainly hustlers. (See also COURTESIES AND SOCIAL CUSTOMS.)

MONEY MATTERS

The currency of Mexico is the **peso**, designated by a dollar sign with only one stroke through it ($). The peso is divided into 100 centavos, but coins lower than 20 pesos are rarely seen since devaluation set the US dollar well above 2,500 pesos. Other coins are 50, 100, 500, 1000, and 5000 pesos. Bills are issued in 2000, 5000, 10,000, 20,000, 50,000 and 100,000.

Banking hours are normally from 9 a.m. to 3 p.m., Monday through Friday, but Banamex branches in the capital stay open until 5 p.m., which may set a trend. In the provinces banks may decline to change money on Friday after 11 a.m. Keep in mind that all banks are crowded on Mondays. There is no black market and the peso floats freely. Keeping pace with inflation that, in 1991, was running about 15% per year, the peso generally decreases in value against the US dollar by about one peso per day, another reason for not cashing more money than you will need in one week. All banks are nationalized. **Private exchange bureaux** (*casas de cambio*) change money at or near bank rates, and are open longer hours and on many holidays. Try to accumulate a store of 100 and 500 peso coins and small bills for tips, taxis and small purchases. Merchants and drivers frequently can't (or won't) make change. Hotels will change money at all hours, but at disadvantageous rates.

Leading **credit cards** are widely accepted throughout Mexico, though not in petrol stations. If you're planning to charge a hotel bill or meal on your credit card, you'd better ask in advance if it will be honoured. When cashing **traveller's checks** you will be asked to show your passport. In airports, border towns and the big beach resorts, US dollars are often widely accepted and prices may even be quoted in dollars.

I want to change some dollars/pounds.	**Quiero cambiar dólares/libras /esterlinas.**
Do you accept traveller's checks?	**¿Acepta usted cheques de viajero?**
Can I pay with this credit card?	**¿Puedo pagar con esta tarjeta de crédito?**
How much?	**¿Cuánto es?**
Have you anything cheaper?	**¿Tiene algo más barato?**

N NEWSPAPERS AND MAGAZINES

An unusual number of daily newspapers are published in Mexico City, most of them heavily oriented toward local and national events. An English daily, the *Mexico City News*, is distributed where tourists are found. Only in the leading hotels and bookstores of the main cities and resorts will you find foreign newspapers and magazines, and these will usually be from the U.S. Often the best way to keep up with the news is through your hotel's TV, which may have US channels.

Have you any English-language newspapers/magazines	**¿Tiene periódicos/revista en iglés?**

PETS AND VETS

Generally speaking, unless you are travelling in a van or trailer, bringing a pet to Mexico is not a good idea. You must produce proof of a recent rabies vaccination and a veterinary health certificate at the border, and you may find that hotel and restaurants will not accept pets. You'll also have problems transporting a pet by air and bus. But vets are in good supply in the major cities. You'll find them listed under *Medicos Veterinarlos Zootecnistas* in the yellow pages of the phone book.

PHOTOGRAPHY

Well-known brands of film are widely available in all varieties. Processing can be done in an hour in big cities and always in a day or two, with the exception of certain diapositive slides. Video cassettes are also in good supply. Remember that the sun is very bright at the coast. You won't need high speed film for most purposes, but the custodians of many artistic and archaeological sites will not allow the use of flash. In quite a few museums, touristic sites and churches you may have to check your camera at the entrance or pay a fee to use it.

I'd like a film for this camera.	**Quisiera un rollo para esta cámara.**
a film for colour pictures	**un rollo en color**
for black-and-white	**en blanco y negro**
for colour-slides	**de transparencias**
35-mm-film	**de treinta y cinco**
super-8	**super ocho**
How long will it take to develop (and print) this film?	**¿Cuánto tardará en revelar (y sacar copias de) este rollo?**
May I take a picture?	**¿Puedo tomar una foto?**

POLICE (*policía*)

There are two branches of the police in Mexico City – the traffic and criminal divisions. Those who speak a foreign language wear rectangular badges showing the flags of the countries whose languages they speak.

Police telephone numbers are different across the country, but for emergencies you can dial **06** everywhere.

PUBLIC HOLIDAYS (*día festivo*)
The Mexican fiesta calendar offers a full array of celebrations to choose from (almost 30), but the official list follows:

January 1	*Año Nuevo*	New Year's Day
February 5	*Aniversario de la Constitución*	Constitution Day
March 21	*Nacimiento de Benito Juárez*	Birthday of Benito Juárez
Movable date	*Pascua ó Semana Santa*	Easter
May 1	*Día del Trabajo*	Labour Day
May 5	*Batalla de Puebla*	Battle of Puebla
September 1	*Informe presidencial*	President's address, 1st day of Congress
September 16	*Día de la Independencia*	Independence Day
October 12	*Día de la Raza*	Columbus Day
November 2	*Día de los Muertos*	All Soul's Day
November 20	*Aniversario de la Revolución*	Anniversary of the Mexican Revolution
December 12	*Nuestra Señora de Guadalupe*	Our Lady of Guadalupe
December 25	*Navidad*	Christmas Day

Are you open tomorrow?	**¿Está abierto mañana?**

 RADIO and TV
Many first-class hotels have dish antennas and cable TV that pick up US programmes and show English-language films. There are numerous Spanish-language radio stations playing music all day. Taxi and bus drivers like it LOUD. Radio VIP (AM 1560) and Stereo Best (FM 105) broadcast some programmes in English.

Three channels, easily found, have been approved by the Mexican ministry for CB radio (citizen's band): one is for communication between individual tourists, a second for intercommunication among recreational vehicles travelling as a caravan, and a third for contacting the tourist highway assistance patrol who can also provide tourist information.

RELIGIOUS SERVICES
Mexico is predominantly Roman Catholic, but there are Protestant evangelical churches in all major cities. In the capital, several Catholic and Protestant churches hold services in English and French. Jewish services are in Hebrew and Spanish. Consult the Friday edition of *The News* for details.

What time is mass/the service?	**¿A qué hora es la misa/eculto?**
Is it in English?	**¿Es en inglés?**

SMOKING (See also CUSTOMS AND ENTRY REGULATIONS).   **S**
You can bring into Mexico 200 cigarettes (*cigarrillos*) or 100 cigars (*puros*). All tobacco (*tabaco*) sold is produced in Mexico, including many US brands made under licence. Cigarettes cost about $1 a packet. Hand-rolled Mexican cigars rivalling the Cuban, cost about 40 cents.

A pack of ...	**Una cajetilla de ...**
filter-tipped	**con filtro**
without filter	**sin filtro**
A box of matches	**Una caja de cerillos**

TAXIS   **T**
Taxis are normally not expensive, but you should definitely ask the driver how much the ride will cost before starting out. Often the meters don't work, and if they do, may not be turned on, and if they are, may give only a base price that must be adjusted for inflation or other reasons from a chart that

may or may not be pasted on a window, and if it is, which you may or may not understand. And so on!

There are several kinds of taxis and they charge different rates. The most expensive are the *turismo* cars, usually new and rather elegant models of any colour, that hang around the better hotels and near museums. The drivers often speak English and solicit tourists as they pass by. They may charge around $10 an hour. The *sitio* cabs operate from cab stands. They are standard yellow cars and charge a bit more than the cruising small cabs, usually two-door VWs with only the back seat for two or three passengers. Airport taxis can only take passengers from the airport to town, not the reverse, and charge a fixed price that is about half what a normal cab fare will legitimately cost when you leave. You can often negotiate a very reasonable deal for the day or for several hours with a regular cab.

What's the fare to ...?	**¿Cuál es la tarifa a ...?**

TIME DIFFERENCE
Most of Mexico is on Central Standard Time (GMT minus 6 hours). It does not change for daylight savings in summer. The states of Baja California Sur, Nayarit, Sinaloa and Sonora are on Mountain Standard Time. Baja California Norte is on Pacific Standard Time.

What time is it?	**¿Qué hora es?**

TIPPING
Wages are low in Mexico and tipping is general, including the maid who does your room, waiters, parking and restroom attendants, barbers, and tour guides. Taxi drivers don't expect a tip, but will be grateful to receive one. 10% is a minimum tip on a restaurant bill, higher in more elaborate establishments. (The tip is sometimes included, so check your bill.) Keep a supply of coins handy for the inevitable tipping and for the indigent elderly who sit outside churches and markets.

Some further guidelines:
Barber/hairdresser	15%
Maid, per week	equivalent of $4–8
Hotel porter, per bag	equivalent of $.25–50

Taxi driver	10% (more after 10 p.m.)
Tourist guide	10% (optional)

Keep the change.	**Déjelo para usted.**

TOILETS

In Mexico the toilets may be referred to as *baños*, *sanitarios*, *tocadores*, *escusados*, *retretes* or *WC*. The doors may be labelled *caballeros* or H (*hombres*) for men, and M (*mujeres*) or *damas* for women. Progress has been made recently in keeping public toilets clean, but carry tissues with you. If there is an attendant, a small tip is expected.

Where are the toilets?	**¿Dónde están los sanitarios?**

TOURIST INFORMATION OFFICES (*oficina de turismo*)

The Mexican government maintains many tourist offices abroad; in addition, any Mexican consulate will provide information about travel to Mexico.

Following is a list of the **Mexican Government Tourism Offices** found throughout Great Britain, Canada and the USA:

USA
70 East Lake Street, Suite 1413, chicago, IL 60601, tel. (312) 606-9015
2707 N. Loop West, Suite 450, Houston, TX 77008, tel. (713) 880-5153
10100 Santa Monica Blvd, Suite 224, Los Angeles, CA 90067,
tel. (213) 203-8191/203-0821
405 Park Ave, Suite 1022, New York, NY 10022, tel. (212) 755-7212/755-4756

Canada
Suite 1801, 2 Sloor Street W., Toronto M4W 3E2, Ontario,
tel. (416) 925-0704/925-1876
Suite 2409, 1 pl. Ville Marie, Montreal, Quebec H3B 3M9, te., (514) 871-1052/871-1057

Great Britain
60/61 Trafalgar Square, London WC2N 5DS; tel. (071) 734-1058

And a partial list of the Tourism Offices in Mexico:
Av. Presidente Masaryk 172, Plolanco, Mexico City, CP 11587,
tel. (5) 250-0123/250-8555
Londres and Amberes 54, Pink Zone, Mexico City, CP06600,
tel. (5) 525-9380, 525-9384
Ignacio Comonfort 2 Altos, Casa de la Campanas, Cuernavaca, Morelos,
CP 62000, tel. (73) 121-815/125-414
Paseo de Gollado 50, Plaza Tapatia, Guadalajara, Jalisco, CP 44100,
tel. (36) 148-665/148-543
Av. Acuaducto 303, Centro, Morelia, Morelos, CP 58000, tel.
(451) 20522/20123/28498
Costera Miguel Alemán 187, Acapulco, Guerrero, CP 39580,
tel. (748) 54128/51022/51304/51249
Centro Internacional, Costera Miguel Alemán, Acapulco, Guerrero, CP
39580, tel. (748) 47050
Edificio Parian de Puente, Local 13, libertad y miramar, Puerto Vallarta,
Jalisco, CP 48300, tel. (322) 22554/22555/22556
Montecinos 220, Between 5 de Mayo and Independencia, Col. Centro,
Veracruz, Veracruz, CP 91700, tel. (29) 327-026
Edificio de la Unidad Administrativa Municipal, Av. Malecon y Francisco
Villa, Ciudad Juárez, Chihuahua, CP 32000, tel. (16) 152-423/146-692
Matamoros 105, Corner Garcia Vigil, Oaxaca, Oaxaca, CP 78000,
tel. (951) 60144/60045
Blvd. Berisario Dominguez 950, 2nd Floor, Edif. Plaza de las Instituciones,
Tuxtla Gutierrez, Chiapas, CP 29000, tel. (961) 24535/25509
Edificio FONATUR, Av. Coba y Nadir, Cancún, Quintana Roo, CP77500,
tel. (988) 43238
Calle 61 No. 470, Corner Calle 54, Col. Centro, Mérida, Yucatán, CP
97000, tel. (99) 149-431/249-542
Paseo Alvaro Obregon 2130, La Paz, Baja California, CP 23000, tel.
(682) 21190/28019

Tourists can also obtain assistance and information by calling the 'Green
Angels' at 250-82-21, Mexico's answer to the Highway Patrol. They can
be helpful way beyond strictly motoring matters. You will also find 'SOS'
solar cell operated telephones on most of the major highways in the republic,
in case of an emergency.

Where is the nearest tourist office?	**¿Dónde está la oficina de turismo la más cercana?**

TRANSPORT (See also DRIVING IN MEXICO)

By air Internal air travel is not that expensive and you'll avoid time-consuming and tiresome bus or train trips. There are a variety of discounts offered – ask a travel agent.

By bus In town and between cities, the average Mexican prefers to travel by bus. The network is well developed for both purposes. For in-town service in Mexico City, there is an unusual diversity of buses running along the main streets of the capital charging different rates. The cheapest are standard buses that stop at fixed locations usually marked by a shelter. They are yellow with '100' marked on their sides: the charge is 400 pesos and you must have the exact fare. This may be the cheapest ride in any big city on earth. Then there are the smaller modern buses and mini-vans (*colectivos*) that also run along fixed routes, with the final destination posted on the windscreen. They pick up and drop off passengers on demand. These are often still called *peseros* in the capital, since they used to charge a single peso. Now the charge is about the equivalent of 15 US cents (the amount in pesos changes with steady inflation). The money and change is passed from hand to hand by passengers to the driver and back.

On long-distance trips, all but the most budget-conscious travellers will prefer the deluxe and first-class buses, which may have reclining seats, air-conditioning and a toilet. They are a great bargain: ten dollars will take you halfway across the country. Buses will stop every three hours or so for relief and food. First-class buses have their own stations (*central de camiones de primera clase*). You must buy tickets in advance for the reserved seats, and these are usually sold only in the station. Information on schedules is available only in the station, too, so if you're planning a bus trip, check the schedules and buy your ticket the day before, or at least early in the day. Mexico City has four first-class bus terminals for lines heading north, south, east or west, but tickets can be reserved at a few central agencies, such as:

Mexicorama, Calle Londres 161, Zona Rosa, Mexico City, CP 06600, tel. (5) 533-2047

Trailways, Av. Morelos 110, Mexico City, tel. (5) 592-3376

Greyhound, Reforma 27, Mexico City, CP 11000, tel. (5) 535-4200 and 535-2618

By train Train travel is not out of the question but you shouldn't be in a rush to get anywhere. It is cheaper than by bus, although the rail network is not as extensive, and it's certainly more relaxing and often more scenic. Some of the major lines have been renovated so the trains will be newer and more comfortable than in the past; between Mexico City and

Guadalajara, Veracruz, Oaxaca, Mérida, and San Miguel de Allende, for example, and the renowned Copper Canyon Express, with stunning scenery along the way, has been fixed up as well. Definitely buy your tickets in advance.

There are essentially 3 classes: **second class** (*segunda*) which is pretty rough, **first class** (*primera*) which is a bit better, and **special first class** (*primera especial* or *numerada*) which is clean with reserved seats, restrooms, drinking water, and often air conditioning or heating. Especially interesting for long hauls are the night trains where you have a good choice of sleeping accommodations, from roomy berths to well-equipped mini-cabins.

For information, ask an informed travel agent or write directly to:

National Railways of Mexico; Passenger Travel Dept.; Buenavista Grand Central Station; Mexico City 06358, Mexico.

W WATER (*agua*)

Water is the most common source of the bacillus (*B. coli*) causing the *turista* tummy troubles. Never drink water from the tap or take ice. Top hotels and restaurants automatically provide purified water. Bottled Mexican mineral water, naturally carbonated, is pure and delicious. Bottled or canned soft drinks and juices are always safe to drink. (See also HEALTH.)

a bottle of mineral water	**una botella de agua mineral**
carbonated/non-carbonated	**con gas/sin gas**

NUMBERS

0	**cero**	19	**diecinueve**
1	**uno**	20	**veinte**
2	**dos**	21	**veintiuno**
3	**tres**	22	**veintidós**
4	**cuatro**	30	**treinta**
5	**cinco**	31	**treinta y uno**
6	**seis**	32	**treinta y dos**
7	**siete**	40	**cuarenta**
8	**ocho**	50	**cincuenta**
9	**nueve**	60	**sesenta**
10	**diez**	70	**setenta**
11	**onze**	80	**ochenta**
12	**doce**	90	**noventa**
13	**trece**	100	**cien**
14	**catorce**	101	**ciento uno**
15	**quince**	102	**ciento dos**
16	**dieciséis**	500	**quinientos**
17	**diecisiete**	1000	**mil**
18	**dieciocho**	10000	**diez mil**

DAYS

Sunday	**domingo**	Thursday	**jueves**
Monday	**lunes**	Friday	**viernes**
Tuesday	**martes**	Saturday	**sábado**
Wednesday	**miércoles**		

MONTHS

January	**enero**	Jult	**julio**
February	**febrero**	August	**agosto**
March	**marzo**	September	**septiembre**
April	**abril**	October	**octubre**
May	**mayo**	November	**noviembre**
June	**junio**	December	**diciembre**

SOME USEFUL EXPRESSIONS

yes/no	**si/no**
please/thankyou	**por favor/gracias**
excuse me/you're welcome	**perdone/de nada**
where/when/how	**dónde/cuándo/cómo**
how long/how far	**cuánto tiempo/a qué distancia**
yesterday/today/tomorrow	**ayer/hoy/mañana**
day/week/month/year	**dia/semana/mes/año**
left/right	**izquierda/derecha**
up/down	**arriba/abajo**
good/bad	**bueno/malo**
big/small	**grande/pequeño**
cheap/expensive	**barato/caro**
hot/cold	**caliente/frio**
old/new	**viejo/nuevo**
open/closed	**abierto/cerrado**
Do you speak English?	**¿Habla usted inglés?**
I don't understand.	**No entiendo.**
Please write it down.	**Por favor, escribalo.**
Help me please.	**Ayúdeme, por favor.**
Get me a doctor – quickly!	**Llamen a un médico, rápido!**
Waiter! Waitress!	**Mesero!/Mesera!**
I'd like ...	**Quisiera ...**
How much is that	**¿Quánto es?**
What time is it?	**¿Qué hora es?**
Where are the toilets?	**¿Dónde están los baños?**

UNITED

Tijuana
Mexicali
Ensenada
San Felipe
Nogales
El Paso
Ciudad Juárez

Desierto de Altar

Sierra San Pedro Mártir

BAJA CALIFORNIA NORTE

SONORA

Hermosillo

CHIHUAHUA

Chihuahua
Cuauhtémoc

Rio Grande

Bahía Sebastián Vizcaíno

Guaymas

Creel

COAHUILA

Parque Natural Ojo de Liebre
Santa Rosalía

Parque Nacional Barranca del Cobre

PACIFIC

Loreto

BAJA CALIFORNIA SUR

Golfo de California

Los Mochis

Sierra Madre Occidental

Torreón

DURANGO

Culiacán

Durango

ZACATECAS

Pichilingue
La Paz

SINALOA

San José del Cabo
San Lucas

Mazatlán

Zacatec

N

0 — 400 km
0 — 240 miles

NAYARIT

San Blas
Compostela

Tepic

Aguascalientes

Guanajua

AGUASCALIENTES

Puerto Vallarta

JALISCO

Ameca

Guadalajara

Leó

Ocotlán
La Ba
Pátzcu

Chapala
L. de Chapala

Colima
COLIMA

El Paracutín
(845m)

Manzanillo

MICHOACÁN

Uruap

MÉXICO STATE

Zihuatanejo

DISTRITO FEDERAL

OCEAN

A. EJIDO

AQUILLES SERDÁN

R. DEL FARALLÓN

A. CUAUHTÉMOC

COSTERA MIGUEL ALEMÁN

Club de Golf

Fuerte de San Diego
Catedral

Centro Cultural y de Convenciónes

La Quebrada

BAHÍA DE ACAPULCO

246

Plaza de Toros

ISLA LA ROQUETA

Punta del Guitarrón

CARRETERA ESCÉNICA

Puerto Marqués

STATES OF AMERICA

MEXICO

Mississippi

New Orleans

Houston

San Antonio

Río Grande

Monterrey
Matamoros

NUEVO
LEÓN

GULF OF MEXICO

Ciudad
Victoria

Tropic of Cancer

TAMAU-
LIPAS

GUANAJUATO

QUERÉTARO

an Luis Potosí
SAN
LUIS
POTOSÍ

HIDALGO

Bahía de Campeche

Progreso
Mérida Izamal
Río Lagartos

Puerto Juárez
Cancún
Cozumel

San Miguel de Allende

YUCATÁN Valladolid

Querétaro

Pachuca
Iztaccíhuatl
(5,286m)

Panantla

orelia
MEXICO

Tlaxcala
Jalapa

TLAXCALA

Campeche

QUINTANA
ROO

CAMPECHE

Toluca
Xochimilco
Cuernavaca
Taxco

Puebla
Cholula
Popocatépetl
(5,452m)
PUEBLA
Acatlán
Teotitlán

Orizaba
Córdoba

Veracruz

VERACRUZ

TABASCO

Chetumal

Villahermosa

Palenque

BELIZE
Golfo
de
Honduras

JERRERO
arque Nacional
Guerrero

Sierra Madre del Sur

Oaxaca
Tlacolula
Ocotlán Mitla

*Istmo
de
Tehuantepec*

Ocosingo

Belmopán

BELIZE

hilpancingo

OAXACA

capulco

MORELOS

Puerto Escondido
Colotepec

Huatulco
Puerto Ángel

Tuxtla
Gutiérrez

San Cristóbal de las Casas
Chiapas
de Corzo

CHIAPAS GUATEMALA

HONDURAS

*Golfo
de
Tehuantepec*

Sierra Madre

GUATEMALA

SAN
SALVADOR
EL
SALVADOR

247

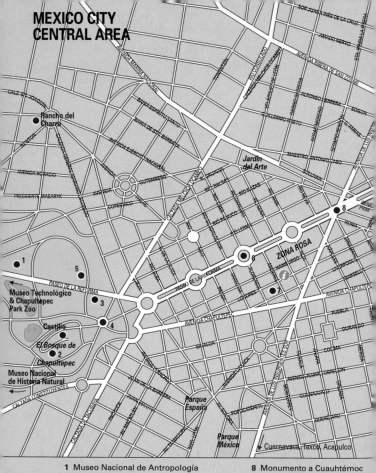

MEXICO CITY CENTRAL AREA

Rancho del Charro

Jardín del Arte

ZONA ROSA

Museo Tecnológico & Chapultepec Park Zoo

Castillo

El Bosque de Chapultepec

Museo Nacional de Historia Natural

Parque España

Parque México

Cuernavaca, Taxco, Acapulco

PASEO DE LA REFORMA

AVENIDA CHAPULTEPEC

1 Museo Nacional de Antropología
2 Galería de Historia
3 Museo de Arte Moderno
4 Monumento a los Niños Héroes
5 Museo Rufino Tamayo
6 Monumento a la Independencia
7 Mercado de Londres

8 Monumento a Cuauhtémoc
9 Monumento a la Revolución
10 Museo de San Carlos
11 Museo Nacional de Arte
12 Pinacoteca Virreinal
13 Mercado Ciudadela
14 Mercado de San Juan

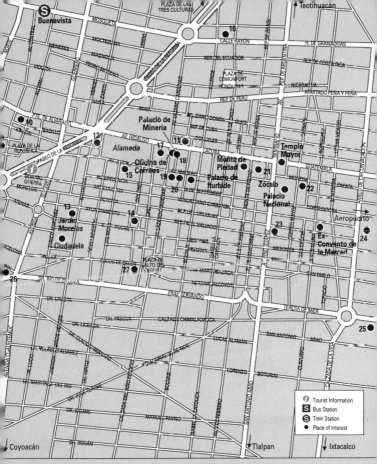

MEXICO, D.F.

N

CIUDAD SATÉLITE

NAUCALPAN

IXTACALA
Tepotzlán
Tula
ZACATENCO

GUADALUPE

Los Indios Verdes

ATZCAPOTZALCO

Toluca

TACUBA

Plaza El Toreo

Hipódromo de las Américas

Zoológica

Bosque y lago San Juan de Aragón

Texcoco

TLATELOLCO

Ⓢ Estación Central

Plaza de las Tres Culturas

Catedral

Palacio Nacional

Zócalo

Aeropuerto Internacional Benito Juárez

Bosque de Chapultepec

Museo Tecnológico

Castillo

Molino del Rey

Museo de Historia Natural

Centro Médico Nacional

Autódromo

AV. CONSTITUYENTES

TACUBAYA

CIUDAD DEPORTIVA

Toluca Guadalajara

MIXCOAC

Polyforum Siqueiros

Estadio Nacional

Plaza México

IXTACALCO

Avenida Río Churubusco

IXTAPALAPA

CULHUACAN

SAN ANGEL

Museo Frida Kahlo

Museo Trotsky

Club de Golf Churubusco

Universidad Ibero-Americana

San Jacinto

Museo Regional de El Carmen

COYOACAN

Tasqueña (Metro terminal)

Estadio Olímpico

El Pedregal

Piscina

Universidad Nacional Autónoma de México

Museo Diego Rivera 'Anahuacal.li'

SAN JERÓNIMO

Estadio Azteca

Ⓢ Train Station
● Place of Interest

TEZONCO

Pirámide de Cuicuilco

CONTRERAS

TLALPAN

0   5 km

0   3 miles

Club de Golf 'México'

Taxco, Chilpancingo, Acapulco

Jardines Flotantes

XOCHIMILCO

OAXACA

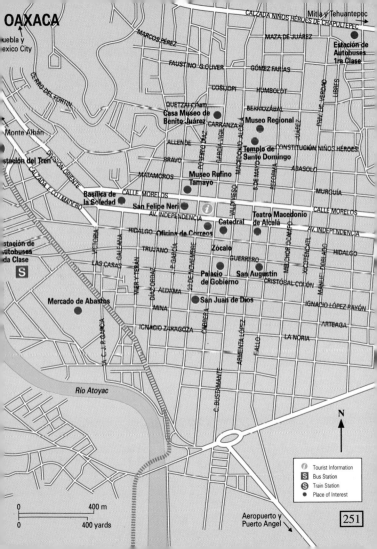

Puebla y
Mexico City

Monte Albán

CERRO DEL FORTIN

estación del Tren

estación de
autobuses
2da Clase

S

CALZADA NIÑOS HÉROES DE CHAPULTEPEC

Mitla y Tehuantepec

MARCOS PEREZ

MAZA DE JUAREZ

Estación de
Autobuses
1ra Clase

FAUSTINO G.OLIVER

GÓMEZ FARIAS

COSIJOPI

HUMBOLDT

QUETZALCOATL

BERRIOZÁBAL

Casa Museo de
Benito Juárez

CARRANZA

Museo Regional

ALLENDE

Templo de
Santo Domingo

CONSTITUCIÓN NIÑOS HÉROES

BRAVO

ABASOLO

MATAMOROS

Museo Rufino
Tamayo

MURGUIA

CALLE MORELOS

Basílica de
la Soledad

San Felipe Neri

AV. INDEPENDENCIA

Catedral

Teatro Macedonio
de Alcalá

CALLE MORELOS

AV. INDEPENDENCIA

HIDALGO

Oficina de Correos

HIDALGO

VICTORIA

GALEANA

TRUJANO

Zócalo

GUERRERO

LAS CASAS

MIER Y TERAN

20 DE NOVIEMBRE

J. P. GARCIA

DIAZ ORDAZ

Palacio
de Gobierno

ALDAMA

San Augustín

CRISTOBAL COLÓN

Mercado de Abastos

MINA

San Juan de Dios

IGNACIO LÓPEZ RAYÓN

IGNACIO ZARAGOZA

ARMENTA LÓPEZ

LA NORIA

ARTEAGA

FALLO

Río Atoyac

C. BUSTAMANTE

N

Aeropuerto y
Puerto Angel

	Tourist Information
S	Bus Station
S	Train Station
●	Place of Interest

251

GUANAJUATO

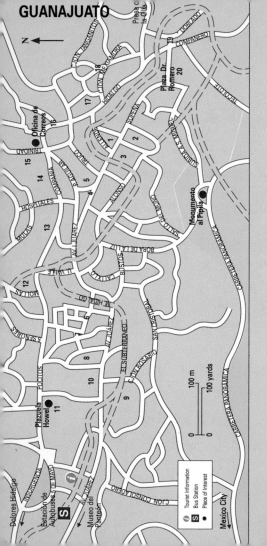

1 Jardín de la Unión
2 Teatro Juárez
3 Iglesia de San Diego
4 Plaza de la Paz
5 Basílica de Nuestra Señora de Guanajuato
6 Plazuela de San Fernando
7 Plazuela San Roque

8 Jardín de la Reforma
9 Mercado Hidalgo
10 Templo de Belén
11 Alhóndiga de Granaditas
12 Casa Diego Rivera
13 Museo del Pueblo de Guanajuato
14 Universidad

15 Iglesia de la Compañía
16 Plazuela del Baratillo
17 Teatro Principal
18 Plaza Mexiamora
19 Plazuela del Ropero
20 Iglesia de San Francisco

Tourist Information
Bus Station
Place of Interest

100 m
100 yards

GUADALAJARA

N

ZAPOPAN

Presa

SECTOR HIDALGO

CALZ. ATEMAJAC

CALZ. MANUEL AVILA CAMACHO

CALZ. VIEJA

S Bus Station

S Train Station

● Place of Interest

Zacatecas

MONTE CASINO

Jalisco Stadium

CIRCUNVALACION

Plaza de Toros

CIRCUNVALACION

SECTOR LIBERTAD

INDUSTRIA

ORTIZ DE DOMINGUEZ

MINA

GIGANTES

SECTOR REFORMA

10 DE SEP

A. PUGA

AV. JUAREZ

WASHINGTON

NIÑOS HEROES

AV. DE LAS TORRES

Parque Agua Azul

CALZ. REVOLUCION

S Terminal de Autobuses

Casa de la Artesanias de Jalisco

Lienzo Charro

Estación del Tren

Mexico City

CALZ. MARIANO OTERO

NIÑO OBRERO

SECTOR JUAREZ

TLAQUEPAQUE

Chapala y Aeropuerto

CENTRAL GUADALAJARA

Parque Morelos

Oficina de Correos

REFORMA

San Felipe Neri

INDEPENDENCIA

Santa Monica

HIDALGO

Plaza de los Laureles

MORELOS

PEDRO MORENO

AV. JUAREZ

LOPEZ COTILLA

Rotonda

Museo

Plaza de la Liberacion

Catedral

Palacio del Gobierno

Plaza de Armas

SANCHEZ

INDUSTRIA

HIDALGO REPUBLICA

Teatro Degollado

Plaza Tapatía

Hospicio Cabañas

ALLENDE

Mercado Libertad

MINA MINA

OBREGON

Plazuela de los Mariachis

GIGANTES

GOMEZ FARIAS

Terminal de Autobuses Estación del Tren

Parque San Francisco

Parque Revolucion

253

INDEX

Where there is more than one set of page references, the one in bold type refers to the main entry.